CONTENTS

D0126950

INTRODUCTION

This *Teach Yourself German Phrasebook* is an essential accessory for travellers of all ages. The main section of the book consists of phrases and sentences organised in a way which will make it easy for you to select the items which will say what YOU want to say.

Start by familiarising yourself with the **Pronunciation Guide** and the **Useful Everyday Phrases**. If you can, practise the phrases you might need beforehand. To help you understand what is being said to you, you will find sections headed *'You may hear'* or *'You may see'* scattered through the book. There is also a **Dictionary** of the most common words and a section of **Essential Information**.

Grammar

German speakers will rarely misunderstand you if you make grammatical mistakes – they will in any case be impressed that you are making an effort to use their language. German is a relatively logical language with few exceptions to its rules. Two short explanations may be useful here:

You German has three words for 'you' to our one. You will notice that all are given in this book, where appropriate. Use as follows:

Sie – polite word for 'you', whether one person or a group; use with anyone you don't know well.

du – informal word for 'you', for just one person; use with a friend, relative, child or animal.

ihr – as for du, but with two or more friends.

In this phrasebook the polite form is denoted by a (P) and the familiar alternative follows in brackets and is denoted by an (F).

The and *a*   English speakers often wonder why there are several words for 'the' and 'a' in German; this is because the basic words **der, die, das** (all of which mean 'the') and **ein, eine** (meaning 'a' or 'an') change their endings according to where they stand in the sentence - rather like 'he' and 'him' or 'they' and 'them' in English.

Gute Reise!

PRONUNCIATION GUIDE

The pronunciation of German is very similar to English and the pronunciation guide for every phrase will allow you to say the German with ease; moreover, letters and combinations of letters in German are always pronounced the same way. The main points to be aware of are as follows:

SYMBOL		GERMAN		ENGLISH
g	*as in*	gerade	*compare with*	**g**et
kh		Loch*		lo**ch**
kv		**Q**uantität		black **v**elvet
s		da**s**		**s**ay
sh		**s**pielen		**sh**ip
ts		**Z**immer		ve**ts**
Y		**j**a		**y**es

z		sie	rose
a		kann	man
aa		fahren	far
ai		wenig	aim
e		wenn	men
ee		wir	seem
ew		Hügel	*see below*
i		bitte	tin
I }	*see*	Eis	I
y }	*below*	leider	fly
o		Woche	not
oh		Person	more
oo		umsteigen	room
ow		laufen	how
oy		heute	boy
ur		möchte	burn

* 'ch' is pronounced 'kh' after a, o, u and au; in all other cases it is pronounced as English 'sh', and is shown as such in this book.

The German letter 'ß' is pronounced 'ss'.

The sound ew (ü) is pronounced as ee, but with the lips rounded as for oo.

The 'y' symbol is generally used to represent the vowel sound in, for example, 'fly'. The 'I' symbol is used at the beginning of words for clarity.

When you see the following letters in written German, they are always pronounced as shown:

sch = *sh*	**v** = v
w = v	**ä** = e or ai
ei = I	**ie** = ee

Stressed syllables are indicated by underlining.

BASIC EXPRESSIONS

THE BASICS

Yes/No	Ja/Nein *Yaa/nyn*
Please/Thank you	Bitte/Danke *bitter/danker*
Excuse me	Entschuldigung *entshooldeegoong*
Can you help me?	Können Sie mir helfen? *kurnen zee meer helfen?*
Good morning/afternoon (evening)	Guten Tag (Abend) *Gooten taag/aabent*
I'm sorry	Es tut mir Leid *Ess toot meer lyt*
Good	Gut *goot*

OK	OK
	okay
That's right	Stimmt
	Shtimmt

ASKING

Where is ...?	Wo ist ...?
	Voh ist ...?
Where can I get ...?	Wo bekomme ich ...?
	Voh berkommer ish ...?
How much is it?	Was kostet das?
	Vas kostet das?
I'd like ...	Ich möchte ...
	ish murshter ...

PROBLEMS, ASKING FOR HELP

I don't know	Ich weiß es nicht
	ish vyss ess nisht
Do you speak English?	Sprechen Sie Englisch?
	shpreshen zee ennglish?
I (don't) understand	Ich verstehe (nicht)
	ish fairshtai-er (nisht)
Do you understand?	Verstehen Sie?
	fairshtai-en zee?
Could you speak slower?	Können Sie bitte langsamer sprechen?
	kurnen zee bitter langsaamer shpreshen?
Could you repeat that?	Können Sie das bitte wiederholen?
	kurnen zee dass bitter veederhohlen?
What does that mean?	Was bedeutet das?
	vas berdoytet das?
Pardon?	Wie bitte?
	vee bitter?

Could you translate this for me?	Könnten Sie mir das übersetzen? *kurnten zee meer das ewberzetsen?*
Could you write that down?	Können Sie das bitte aufschreiben? *kurnen zee dass bitter owf-shryben?*
I can't speak (much) German	Ich spreche kein/wenig Deutsch *ish spresher kyn/wainig doych*
I've lost my way	Ich habe mich verlaufen *ish haaber mish fairlowfen*
Where is the British Embassy/ Consulate?	Wo ist die britische Botschaft/ das britische Konsulat? *voh ist dee britisher bohtshaft/ das britisher konzoolaat?*

GREETINGS AND MAKING FRIENDS

Meeting people

Two sorts of phrases are provided here:

The first, marked **P** (= Polite) uses the more formal word for 'you' (*Sie*); adults talking to adults, or young people talking to adults they don't know, should use this list initially.

The second, marked **F** (= Familiar), uses the familiar *du* for 'you', and is used by teenagers, and by friends of any age.

Good morning	Guten Morgen *gooten morgen*
Good afternoon	Guten Tag *gooten taag*

It's not difficult to make friends in Germany.
It will be especially appreciated if you try to do so in German!

Good evening	Guten Abend *gooten aabent*
Goodbye (in person)	Auf Wiedersehen *owf veederzai-en*
(on phone)	Auf Wiederhören *owf veederhuren*
Bye!	Tschüs! *chewss!*
What's your name?	(P) Wie heißen Sie? *vee hysen zee?*
	(F) Wie heißt du? *vee hyst doo?*
My name is …	Ich heiße … *ish hyser …*
How are you?	(P) Wie geht es Ihnen? *vee gait es eenen?*
	(F) Wie geht's? *vee gaits?*
Fine, thanks. And you?	(P) Gut, danke. Und Ihnen? *goot, danker. oont eenen?*
	(F) Gut, danke. Und dir? *goot, danker. oont deer?*
Pleased to meet you	Freut mich *froyt mish*
Where are you staying at the moment?	(P) Wo wohnen Sie zur Zeit? *voh vohnen zee tsoor tsyt?*
	(F) Wo wohnst du zur Zeit? *voh vohnst doo tsoor tsyt?*
I'm staying…	Ich wohne… *ish vohner…*
Where do you come from?	(P) Woher kommen Sie? *voh-hair kommen zee?*
	(F) Woher kommst du? *voh-hair kommst doo?*

I'm from...	Ich komme aus... *ish kommer ows...*
...America	...Amerika *amerika*
...Australia	...Australien *owstraalien*
...Britain	...Großbritannien *grohs-britaanien*
...Canada	...Kanada *kanada*
...Ireland	...Irland *eerlant*
...Scotland	...Schottland *shotlant*
...Wales	...Wales *vaylz*
I'm a businessman/ businesswoman	Ich bin Geschäftsmann/ Geschäftsfrau *ish bin gersheftsmann/ gersheftsfrow*
I'm a student	Ich bin Student *ish bin shtoodent*
I'm on holiday	Ich bin auf Urlaub *ish bin owf oorlowp*
I'm single/married/divorced	Ich bin verheiratet/ledig/ geschieden *ish bin fairhyrartert/laidig/ gersheeden*
I (don't) like playing tennis	Ich spiele (nicht) gern Tennis *ish shpeeler (nisht) gairn tennis*
Do you like it here?	(P) Gefällt es Ihnen hier? *gerfelt es eenen heer?*
	(F) Gefällt es dir hier? *gerfelt es deer heer?*

Are you here on holiday?	(P) Sind Sie auf Urlaub hier? *zint zee owf oorlowp heer?*
	(F) Bist du auf Urlaub hier? *bist doo owf oorlowp heer?*
I'm on a business trip	Ich bin auf Geschäftsreise *ish bin owf gersheftsryzer*
I work for...	Ich arbeite bei... *ish aarbyter by...*
Are you on your own?	(P) Sind Sie allein? *zint zee alyn?*
	(F) Bist du allein? *bist doo alyn?*
My ... is here too	... ist auch hier *ist owkh heer*
...boyfriend	Mein Freund... *myn froynt...*
...brother	Mein Bruder... *myn brooder...*
...family	Meine Familie... *myner fameeli-er...*
...father	Mein Vater... *myn faater...*
...girlfriend	Meine Freundin... *myner froyndin...*
...husband	Mein Mann... *myn man...*
...mother	Meine Mutter... *myner mooter...*
...parents	Meine Eltern... *myner eltern...*
...sister	Meine Schwester... *myner shvester...*

...wife

Meine Frau...
myner frow...

Do you have a light please?

(P) Haben Sie Feuer, bitte?
haaben zee foyer, bitter?
(F) Hast du Feuer, bitte?
hast doo foyer, bitter?

Would you like a cigarette?

(P) Möchten Sie eine Zigarette?
murshten zee I-ner tsigaretter?

(F) Möchtest du eine Zigarette?
murshtest doo I-ner tsigaretter?

I'm afraid I don't/haven't

Leider nicht
lyder nisht

Would you like a drink?

(P) Möchten Sie etwas trinken?
murshten zee etvas trinken?

(F) Möchtest du etwas trinken?
murshtest doo etvas trinken?

I'd like

ich möchte...
ish murshter...

Nothing for me, thanks

Nichts für mich, danke
nishts fewr mish, danker

Cheers!

Prost!
prohst!

AT RECEPTION

My name is...

Ich heiße...
ish hysser...

I have an appointment with
Mr./Ms. ...

Ich habe eine
Verabredung mit
Herrn/Frau ...
*ish haaber I-ner
fairapraidoong mit
hairn/frow ...*

I'd like to see Mr/Ms ...

Ich möchte Herrn/Frau ...
sprechen
*ish murshter hairn/frow ...
sphreshen*

You may hear:

Vorsicht!
fohrzisht!

Careful! Watch out!

Bitte schön?
bitter shurn?

May I help you?

Bitte schön
bitter shurn

Here you are/you're
welcome

Moment, bitte.
moment, bitter

Wait a moment, please

Danke, gleichfalls
danker, glyshfalls

And the same to you

Ich bin hier fremd
ish bin heer fremt

I'm a stranger here

SIGNS AND NOTICES

Ausfahrt	Exit (vehicles)
Aufzug	Lift
Ausgang	Exit
Auskunft	Information
außer ...	except for ...
Außer Betrieb	Out of order
Belegt	No vacancies
Besetzt	Occupied
Bitte nicht stören	Do not disturb
Damen	Ladies
Drücken	Push
Einfahrt	Entrance (vehicles)

In German, the title for all adult women, married or single, is *Frau*. *Fräulein* is rarely used.

Eingang	Entrance
Eintritt frei	Entrance fee
Erdgeschoss	ground floor
Feiertag	public holiday
Fußgänger	pedestrians
Gefahr	Danger
Geschlossen	Closed
Heiß	Hot
Herren	Men
Kalt	Cold
Kasse	Till/cash desk
Kein Zutritt	No entry
nicht ...	do not ...
Nicht berühren	Do not touch
Nicht rauchen	no smoking
Notausgang	Emergency exit
Notruf	Emergency phone
nur ...	... only
Öffnungszeiten	hours of opening
Rauchen verboten	No smoking
Selbstbedienung	Self-service
Stammtisch	Table reserved for regular customers
Stock	floor, storey
Tiefgeschoss	basement
Ziehen	Pull
Zimmer frei	Vacancies
Zu verkaufen	For sale
Zu vermieten	For hire/rent

Are you waiting for someone?	(P) Warten Sie auf jemanden?
	vaarten zee owf yaimanden?
	(F) Wartest du auf jemanden?
	vaartest doo owf yaimanden?
Are you free this evening?	(P) Haben Sie heute Abend Zeit?
	haaben zee hoyter aabent tsyt?
	(F) Hast du heute Abend Zeit?
	hast doo hoyter aabent tsyt?
I'm sorry, I'm not	Leider nicht
	lyder nisht
How about tomorrow?	Und morgen?
	oont morgen?
Would you like to go to a club?	(P) Möchten Sie in eine Disko gehen?
	murshten zee in I-ner disko gai-en?
	(F) Möchtest du in eine Disko gehen?
	murshtest doo in I-ner disko gai-en?
Would you like to come with me/us?	(P) Kommen Sie mit?
	kommen zee mit?
	(F) Kommst du mit?
	koomst doo mit?
Would you like to go for a drink?	(P) Möchten Sie etwas trinken gehen?
	murshten zee etvas trinken gai-en?
	(F) Möchtest du etwas trinken gehen?
	murshtest doo etvas trinken gai-en?

Yes, I would	Ja, gerne *Yaa, gairner*
I'd rather...	Ich würde lieber... *ish vewrder leeber...*
Where shall we meet?	Wo treffen wir uns? *voh treffen veer oons?*
At what time?	Um wie viel Uhr? *oom veefeel oor?*
I'll pick you up	(P) Ich hole Sie ab *ish hohler zee ab* (F) Ich hole dich ab *ish hohler dish ab*
What is your address/phone number?	(P) Wie ist Ihre Adresse/Telefonnummer? *vee ist eerer adresser/telefohn-noomer?* (F) Wie ist deine Adresse/Telefonnummer? *vee ist dyner adresser/telefohn-noomer?*
Would you like to come over?	(P) Möchten Sie zu uns kommen? *murshten ze tsoo oons kommen?* (F) Möchtest du zu uns kommen? *murshtest doo tsoo oons kommen?*

ARRIVAL AND DEPARTURE

- This section deals with arriving and departing in German-speaking countries. For information on travel (by air, or by public transport), see page 51, taxis and car hire pages 62–64.

- See also buying tickets, page 50.

- Watch out for the following differences in place names:

Basle = Basel
Black Forest = Schwarzwald
Cologne = Köln
Geneva = Genf
Lake Constance = Bodensee

Munich = München
Nuremburg = Nürnberg
Vienna = Wien
River Rhine = der Rhein
River Danube = die Donau
Baltic Sea = die Ostee
The Channel = der Kanal
Bavaria = Bayern

Names of other towns in German-speaking countries are spelt similarly in both English and German.

PASSPORT CONTROL

I'm here on business	Ich bin geschäftlich hier *ish bin gersheftlish heer*
We're here on holiday	Wir sind auf Urlaub hier *veer zint owf oorlowp heer*
I'm/we're staying...	Ich bleibe/wir bleiben... *ish blyber/veer blyben...*
...for 2 days	...zwei Tage *tsvy taager*
...for 1 week/2 weeks	...eine Woche/zwei Wochen *I-ner vokher/tsvy vokhen*
...for 1 month/2 months	...einen Monat/zwei Monate *I-nern mohnaat/tsvy mohnaater*
...till...	...bis zum... *...bis tsoom...*

• See page 158 for dates

We're going...	Wir fahren... *veer faaren...*
...to the Alps	...in die Alpen *in dee alpen*

...to Austria	...nach Österreich
	nakh ursterykh
...to Germany	...nach Deutschland
	nakh doychlant
...to Switzerland	...in die Schweiz
	in dee shvyts

CUSTOMS

• If you have something to declare, go through the red exit (Anmeldepflichtige Waren); otherwise choose the green exit (Anmeldefreie Waren).

I've nothing to declare	Ich habe nichts zu verzollen
	ish haaber nishts tsoo fairtsolen
Do I have to delcare this?	Muss ich das verzollen?
	moos ish das fairtsolen?
How much do I have to pay?	Wie viel muss ich zahlen?
	veefeel moos ish tsaalen?
I've got...	Ich habe...
	ish haaber...
...cigarettes	...Zigaretten
	tsigareten
...cigars	...Zigarren
	tsigaren
...tobacco	...Tabak
	tabak
...spirits	...Spirituosen
	shpiritoo-ohzen
...wine	...Wein
	vyn
...perfume	...Parfüm
	parfung
Here's the receipt	Hier ist die Quittung
	heer ist dee kvittoong

It's a present	Es ist ein Geschenk
	es ist I-n gershenk
Here's my ticket	Hier ist meine Fahrkarte
	heer ist myner faarkaarter
My name is...	Ich heiße...
	ish hysser...
My flight number is...	Meine Flugnummer ist...
	myner floognummer ist...
Here's my address...	Hier ist meine Adresse...
	heer ist myner adresser...

You may hear:

Ihren Pass bitte	Your passport, please
eeren pass bitter	
Wohin fahren Sie?	Where are you travelling to?
voh-hin faaren zee?	
Wie lange bleiben Sie?	How long are you staying?
vee langer blyben zee?	
Bitte öffnen Sie...	Please open...
bitter urfnen zee...	
Haben Sie etwas zu verzollen?	Do you have anything to
haaben zee etvas tsoo fairtsollen?	declare?
Dies ist zollpflichtig	You must pay duty on this
deez ist tsollpflishtig	

You may see:

Abfahrt	Departures
Ankunft	Arrivals
Fluggäste/Passagiere	Passengers
Fluglinie	Airline
Gepäckausgabe	Luggage reclaim
Inland	Internal (flights)
Passkontrolle	Passport control

Zoll	Customs
Zollfreie Waren	Duty-free shop

LUGGAGE

Where are the luggage trolleys?	Wo sind die Kofferkulis? *voh zint dee koffer-kooliz?*
Where do we collect our luggage?	Wo holen wir unser Gepäck ab? *voh hohlen veer oonzer gerpek ap?*
Where's the information desk?	Wo ist die Auskunft? *voh ist dee owskoonft?*
There's a bag/case missing	Eine Tasche/Ein Koffer fehlt *I-ner tascher/I-n koffer failt*
My luggage hasn't arrived yet	Mein Gepäck ist noch nicht da *myn gerpek ist nokh nisht daa*
I can't find my luggage	Ich finde mein Gepäck nicht *ish finder myn gerpek nisht*
Has the luggage from the London flight arrived yet?	Ist das Gepäck von dem Flug aus London schon da? *ist das gerpek fon daim floog ows london shohn daa?*
When will my luggage arrive?	Wann kommt mein Gepäck? *van kommt myn gerpek?*
Could you please find out where my luggage is?	Können Sie bitte herausfinden, wo mein Gepäck ist? *kurnen zee bitter herowsfinden, voh myn gerpek ist?*
I'm leaving for ... tomorrow/ in two days' time	Ich fahre morgen/in zwei Tagen nach ... *ish faarer morgen/in tsvy taagen nakh...*

• Airports and railway stations have luggage trolleys (*Kofferkulis*), for which a small sum may be payable.

DEPARTURE

Here is my ticket/boarding card	Hier ist meine Fahrkarte/meine Bordkarte *heer ist myner faarkaarter/myner bordkaarter*
Can I take this on board?	Kann ich das mit an Bord nehmen? *kan ish das mit an bord naimen?*
How much must I pay for the excess?	Was muss ich für das Übergewicht zahlen? *vas moos ish fewr das ewbergervikht tsaalen?*
From which gate does our flight leave?	Von welchem Flugsteig fährt unser Flug? *fon velshem floogshtyg fairt oonzer floog?*
Has flight (BA960) been called?	Wurde Flug (BA960) schon aufgerufen? *voorder floog (bai aa noyn zekhs nool) shohn owfgeroofen?*
Can I book a seat on another/the next flight?	Kann ich einen Platz für einen anderen Flug/den nächsten Flug reservieren? *kan ish I-nen plats fewr I-nen anderen floog/dain neshsten floog rezairveeren?*
I've missed my...	Ich habe ... verpasst *ish haabe...fairpast*
...plane	...meinen Flug... *mynen floog*

...connection

...meinen Anschluss...
mynen anshlooss...

...coach/bus

...meinen Bus...
mynen boos

...train

...meinen Zug...
mynen tsoog

...ferry

...meine Fähre...
myner fairer

You may hear:

Der Flug nach...hat...
Minuten Verspätung
*dair floog nakh...hat...
minooten fairshpaitoong*

The flight to...will be...
minutes late

ACCOMMODATION

HOTELS AND YOUTH HOSTELS

• *Zimmer frei* indicates that there are vacancies. *Belegt* or *Besetzt* indicates that all the rooms are taken.

• The choice of accommodation is usually between the following:

Hotel (garni)	hotel (bed and breakfast)
Gasthaus/Gasthof	inn

 If you have not made a booking before your arrival, there are several ways of finding a room. Look out for: *Zimmernachweis* or *Zimmervermittlung*: a room-booking service at airports or major stations. *Fremdenverkehrsbüro* or *Fremdenverkehrsamt*: the tourist information office, which offers a similar service.

Pension/Fremdenheim	guest house
Jugendherberge	youth hostel

BOOKING A ROOM

Do you have an accommodation list?	Haben Sie ein Hotelverzeichnis? *haaben zee I-n hohtel-fair-tsyshniss?*
Can you reserve a room for me/us?	Können Sie mir/uns ein Zimmer reservieren? *kurnen zee meer/oons I-n tsimmer reserveeren?*
...in a hotel	...in einem Hotel *in I-nem hohtel*
...in a guest house	...in einer Pension *in I-ner penziohn*
...in the town centre	...in der Stadtmitte *in dair shtat-mitter*
...near the airport/station	...in der Nähe vom Flughafen/Bahnhof *in dair nai-er fom flooghafen/baanhohf*
...for 1/2 nights	...für eine Nacht/zwei Nächte *fewr I-ner nakht/tsvy neshter*
I'm not sure yet how long we'll stay	Ich weiß noch nicht, wie lange wir bleiben *ish vys nokh nisht, vee langer veer blyben*
Do you have anything cheaper/better?	Haben Sie etwas Billigeres/Besseres? *haaben zee etvas biligeres/besseres?*
How do I get there?	Wie komme ich dahin? *vee komer ish dahin?*

Can you show me on a street map?	Können Sie es mir auf einem Stadtplan zeigen?
	kurnen zee es meer owf I-nem shtat-plan tsygen?
What does it cost...?	Was kostet es...?
	vas kostet es...?
...per night	...pro Nacht
	proh nakht
...with breakfast	...mit Frühstück
	mit frewstewk
...with full/half board	...mit Vollpension/Halbpension
	mit follpenziohn/halp-penziohn
...for children	...für Kinder
	fewr kinder
Does that include breakfast/VAT?	Ist das mit Frühstück/Mehrwertsteuer?
	ist das mit frewstewk/mairvairt-shtoyer?
That's too expensive	Das ist mir zu teuer
	das ist meer tsoo toyer
I'd like a single room...	Ich möchte ein Einzelzimmer...
	ish murshter I-n I-ntseltsimmer...
We'd like a double room/twin room...	Wir möchten ein Doppelzimmer/Zweibettzimmer...
	veer murshtun I-n doppel-tsimmer/tsvy-bet-tsimmer...
...with a bath	...mit Bad
	mit baat
...with a shower	...mit Dusche
	mit doosher
...with a balcony	...mit Balkon
	mit balkohn

Does it have cable/satellite TV?	Hat es Kabel-/ Satellitenfernsehen? *hat es kaabel/ zaturleeten-fairnsaihen?*
Do you have any vacancies?	Haben Sie ein Zimmer frei? *haaben zee I-n tsimmer fry?*
I/we have a reservation	Ich habe/wir haben ein Zimmer reserviert *ish haaber/veer haaben I-n tsimmer rezerveert*
My name is...	Ich heiße... *ish hyser...*
May I see the room?	Darf ich das Zimmer sehen? *daarf ish das tsimmer sai-en?*
It's too small/noisy	Es ist zu klein/laut *es ist tsoo klyn/lowt*
Can we have a child's cot?	Können wir ein Kinderbett haben? *kurnen veer I-n kinnderbet haaben?*
Could you have my luggage brought to my room?	Können Sie bitte mein Gepäck auf mein Zimmer bringen lassen? *kurnten zee bitter myn gerpek owf myn tsimmer bringen lassen?*
Where can I park my car?	Wo kann ich mein Auto parken? *voh kan ish myn owtoh parken?*
We'll take it	Wir nehmen es *veer naimen es*

You may see:

Rezeption	
Empfang	Reception
Anmeldung	
Abendessen	evening meal
Aufzug/Fahrstuhl	lift
belegt	no vacancies
Eingang	entrance
Erdgeschoss	ground floor
erster Stock	first floor
Frühstück	breakfast
Halbpension	half board
kein Zutritt	no entry
Mittagessen	lunch
nur für Gäste	patrons only
Rechnung	bill
Vollpension	full board
Zimmer frei	vacancies
Name	name
Vorname	forename
Nummer	number
Straße	road
Wohnort	town
Postleitzahl (Plz)	postcode
Geburtsdatum	date of birth
Geburtsort	place of birth
Passnummer	passport number
Datum	date
Unterschrift	signature

You will often be asked to fill in a registration form (*Anmeldeformular*).

You may hear:

Wir haben kein Zimmer mehr frei *veer haaben kyn tsimmer mair fry*	We have no more rooms free
Wir sind voll belegt *veer sint foll berlaigt*	We're full up
Wir haben keine Doppelzimmer mehr frei *veer haaben kyner dopel-tsimmer mair fry*	We have no double rooms free
Wie heißen Sie? *vee hyssen zee?*	What is your name?
Bitte füllen Sie das Anmeldeformular aus *bitter fewlen zee das anmelder-formoolaar ows*	Please fill in the registration form
Darf ich Ihren Pass sehen? *daarf ish eeren pass sai-en?*	May I see your passport?
Unterschreiben Sie, bitte *oontershryben zee, bitter*	Please sign this
Wie lange bleiben Sie? *vee langer blyben zee?*	How long are you staying?
Ihre Zimmernummer ist... *eerer tsimmer-noomer ist...*	Your room number is...

Das Zimmer ist im...
    ...Erdgeschoss
    ...ersten Stock
das tsimmer ist im ...
    ...airdgeshoss
    ...airsten shtock
	The room is on the...
	    ...ground floor
	    ...first floor

Nehmen Sie den Aufzug *naimen zee dain owftsoog*	Take the lift

ROOM SERVICE AND MEALS

What time is breakfast/ evening meal?	Wann gibt es Frühstück/ Abendessen? *van gipt ess frewstewk/ aabentessen?*
Can we have breakfast in our room?	Können wir auf unserem Zimmer frühstücken? *kurnen veer owf oonzerem tsimmer frewstewkern?*
Please wake me at ... o'clock	Bitte wecken Sie mich um ... Uhr *bitter veken zee mish um ... oor*
May I have...?	Könnte ich ... haben? *kurnter ish ... haaben?*
...a bath towel	...ein Badetuch *I-n baadertookh*
...some clothes hangers	...einige Kleiderbügel *I-niger klyderbewgel*
...another pillow	...noch ein Kopfkissen *nokh I-n kopf-kissen*
...some soap	...Seife *zyfer*
...an ashtray	...einen Aschenbecher *I-nen ashen-bekher*
...an extra blanket	...eine extra Decke *I-ner extra dekker*
...a needle and thread	...eine Nadel und etwas Faden *I-ner naadel oont etvas faaden*
Can you get me a taxi?	Können Sie mir ein Taxi bestellen? *kurnen zee meer I-n taxi bershtellen?*

Can I phone direct from my room?	Kann ich von meinem Zimmer durchwählen? *kan ish von mynem tsimmer doorkh-vailen?*
Is there any post for me?	Ist Post für mich da? *ist posst fewr mish daa?*
My room number is...	Meine Zimmernummer ist... *myner tsimmer-noomer ist...*
What is my room number?	Welche Zimmernummer habe ich? *velscher tsimmer-noomer haaber ish?*
Could I have my key please?	Den Schlüssel, bitte *dain shlewssel bitter*
Can I leave this in the safe?	Kann ich das im Safe deponieren? *kan ish das im 'safe' deponeeren?*
I want these clothes cleaned/washed	Ich möchte diese Kleider reinigen/waschen lassen *ish murshter deezer klyder rynigern/vashern lassen*
I need them today/tonight/tomorrow	Ich brauche sie heute/heute Abend/Morgen *ish browkher zee hoyter/hoyter aabent/morgen*
Are there any messages for me?	Hat jemand eine Nachricht für mich hinterlassen? *hat Yaimant I-ner nakh-risht fewr mish hinterlassen?*
Is there room service?	Gibt es Zimmerservice? *gipt es tsimmer-surrvis?*

QUERIES AND COMPLAINTS

The...is broken/doesn't work/is blocked	...funktioniert nicht/ist kaputt/ist verstopft *foonktsioneert nisht/ist kapoot/ist fairshtopft*
...heating...	Die Heizung... *dee hytsoong...*
...light...	Das Licht... *das lisht...*
...plug (electric)...	Der Stecker... *dair shteker...*
...shutter...	Der Fensterladen... *dair fenster-laaden...*
...shower...	Die Dusche... *dee doosher...*
...socket...	Die Steckdose... *dee shtekdohzer...*
...television...	Der Fernseher... *dair fairnzai-er...*
...wash-basin...	Das Waschbecken... *das vashbeken...*
...bath...	Die Badewanne... *dee baadervanner...*
...toilet...	Die Toilette... *dee twaletter...*
...air conditioning...	Die Klimaanlage... *dee kleema-anlaager...*
...radio...	Das Radio... *das raadio...*
How does ... work?	Wie funktioniert...? *vee foonktsioneert...?*
The window is jammed	Das Fenster klemmt *das fenster klemmt*

The tap is dripping	Der Wasserhahn tropft *dair vasserhaan tropft*
The bulb has blown	Die Birne ist kaputt *dee beerner ist kapoot*
My room has not been cleaned	Mein Zimmer wurde nicht gereinigt *myn tsimmer voorder nisht ger-ynikt*
Can you get it repaired?	Können Sie es reparieren lassen? *kurnen zee es repareeren lassen?*
There isn't any hot water	Es gibt kein warmes Wasser *es gipt kyn vaarmes vasser*
Where is the...?	Wo ist...? *voh ist...?*
...dining-room	...der Speisesaal...? *dair shpyzer-zaal...?*
...lift	...der Fahrstuhl *dair faar-shtool*
...toilet	...die Toilette *dee twaletter*
Do you have any...?	Haben Sie...? *haaben zee...?*
...writing paper	...Schreibpapier *shryp-papeer*
...envelopes	...Briefumschläge *breef-oomshlaiger*
...stamps	...Briefmarken *breefmaarken*
Can I make a phone call from here?	Kann ich von hier telefonieren? *kan ish fon heer telefohneeren?*

CHECKING OUT

May I have the bill?	Können Sie mir bitte die Rechnung geben? *kurnen zee meer bitter dee reshnoong gaiben?*
Can I pay by credit card?	Kann ich mit Kreditkarte bezahlen? *kan ish mit kredeet-karter bertsaalen?*
I'm/we're leaving...	Ich fahre/wir fahren...ab *ish faarer/veer faaren...ap*
...tomorrow	...morgen... *morgen...*
...today	...heute... *hoyter...*
Can we have our luggage brought down?	Können Sie unser Gepäck herunterbringen lassen? *kurnen zee oonzer gerpek hairoonter-bringen lassen?*
I must leave at once	Ich muss sofort abreisen *ish moos zofort ap-ryzen*
Is everything included?	Ist alles inbegriffen? *ist alles inbergriffen?*
I think you've made a mistake (in the bill)	Ich glaube, Sie haben sich verrechnet *ish glowber zee haaben zish fair-rekhnet*
Can you call a taxi?	Können Sie bitte ein Taxi rufen? *kurnen zee bitter I-n taxi roofen?*
Here's the forwarding address	Hier ist meine Nachsendeadresse *heer ist myner nakh-zender-adresser*
I'm in a hurry	Ich habe es eilig *ish haaber es I-lig*

YOUTH HOSTEL

• There are separate dormitories for men and women, and you are advised to take your own sleeping bag.

Where is the youth hostel?	Wo ist die Jugendherberge, bitte? *voh ist dee Yoogent-hairbairger, bitter?*
Do you have any beds free?	Haben Sie noch Plätze frei? *haaben zee nokh pletser fry?*
We'd like to stay 1/2 nights	Wir möchten eine Nacht/zwei Nächte bleiben *veer murshten I-ner nakht/tsvy neshter blyben*
There's...	Wir sind... *veer zint...*
...1/2 boys	...ein Junge/zwei Jungen *I-n Yoonger/tsvy Yoongen*
...1/2 girls	...ein/zwei Mädchen *I-n/tsvy maidshen*
...1/2 adults	...ein Erwachsener/zwei Erwachsene *I-n/tsvy airvakhsener*
...1/2 children	...ein Kind/zwei Kinder *I-n kint/tsvy kinder*
Here's my membership card	Hier ist mein Ausweis *heer ist myn owsvys*
We need bed linen	Wir brauchen Bettwäsche *veer browkhen betvesher*

We'd like supper and breakfast	Wir möchten Abendbrot und Frühstück *veer murshten aabentbroht oont frewstewk*
Where is...?	Wo ist...? *voh ist...?*
...our dormitory	...unser Schlafraum *oonzer shlaafrowm*
...the kitchen	...die Küche *dee kewsher*
...the shower	...die Dusche *dee doosher*
...the toilet	...die Toilette *dee twaletter*
...the washroom	...der Waschraum *dair vashrowm*

You may hear:

Wir sind voll belegt *veer zint fol berlaigt*	We're full up
Wie viele Personen? *veefeeler pairzohnen?*	How many people?
Wie viele Nächte? *veefeeler neshter?*	How many nights?
Wie lange wollen Sie bleiben? *vee langer vollen zee blyben?*	How long do you want to stay?
Ihren (Ihre) Ausweis(e) bitte *eeren(eerer) owsvyz(er), bitter*	May I have your passport(s) please?
Möchten Sie Bettwäsche leihen? *murshten zee bet-vesher lyen?*	Do you want bed linen?
Welche Mahlzeiten wollen Sie? *velsher maaltsyten vollen zee?*	Which meals do you want?

It is illegal to camp without permission.

CAMPING AND CARAVANNING

• There are thousands of campsites in Germany, Austria and Switzerland. Some, in mountain areas, are open all year round. The tourist office can help you to find a suitable site.

We're looking for a campsite	Wir suchen einen Campingplatz *veer zookhen I-nen kemping-plats*
Can we camp here?	Können wir hier zelten? *kurnen veer heer tselten?*
Are there any other campsites nearby?	Gibt es noch andere Campingplätze in der Nähe? *gipt es nokh anderer kemping-pletser in dair nai-er?*
Do you have any vacancies for…?	Haben Sie Platz für…? *haaben zee plats fewr…?*
…a tent?	…ein Zelt *I-n tselt*
…a caravan	…einen Wohnwagen *I-nen vohnvaagen*
…a motor-home	…ein Wohnmobil *I-n vohn-mobeel*
How much does it cost for…?	Wie viel kostet es für…? *veefeel kostet es fewr…?*
…a night	…eine Nacht *I-ner nakht*
…a week	…eine Woche *I-ner vokher*
…one person	…eine Person *I-ner pairsohn*
…a car	…ein Auto *I-n owtoh*

Does that include everything?	Ist alles im Preis inbegriffen? *ist ales im prys inbergriffen?*
Is/are there...?	Gibt es...? *gipt es...?*
...cooking facilities	...Kochgelegenheiten *kokh-gerlaigenhyten*
...electricity	...Stromanschluss *shtrohm-anshloos*
...shop	...einen Laden *I-nen laaden*
...showers	...Duschen *dooshen*
...a swimming pool	...ein Schwimmbad *I-n shvimbaad*
...washing machines	...Waschmaschinen *vashmasheenen*
Where can I get butane gas?	Wo kann ich Butangas bekommen? *voh kan ish bootaangas berkommen?*
Are there discounts for children?	Gibt es Rabatt für Kinder? *gipt es rabat fewr kinnder?*
Do you have...?	Haben Sie...? *haaben zee...?*
...ice	...Eis *I-s*
...gas	...Butangas *bootaangas*
Does the campsite close at night?	Schließt der Campingplatz nachts? *shleest dair kemping-plats nakhts?*
We're leaving today/tomorrow	Wir fahren heute/morgen ab *veer faaren hoyter/mohrgen ab*

VILLAS & APARTMENTS

• Cleaning is always included in the price.

I'd like an apartment...	Ich möchte eine Ferienwohnung... *ish mu̱rshter I̱-ner fa̱irien vo̱hnoong...*
...with one bedroom	...mit einem Schlafzimmer *mit I̱-nem shla̱af-tsimmer*
...with two bedrooms	...mit zwei Schlafzimmern *mit tsvy shla̱af-tsimmern*
...for four people	...für vier Personen *fewr feer pairzo̱hnen*
...for a week	...für eine Woche *fewr I̱-ner vo̱kher*
...for a fortnight	...für zwei Wochen *fewr tsvy vo̱khen*
Which floor is it on?	In welchem Stock ist es? *in ve̱lshem shtok ist es?*
Is...included?	Ist...inbegriffen? *ist...i̱nbergriffen*
...everything...	...alles... *a̱ll-es...*
...the gas...	...das Gas... *das ga̱s...*
...the water...	...das Wasser... *das va̱sser...*
...the electricity...	...der Strom... *dair shtro̱hm...*
When...?	Wann...? *van...?*
...is it cleaned	...wird geputzt *veert gerpo̱otst*

...is the rubbish collected
...kommt die Müllabfuhr
kommt dee mewl-apfoor

Does it have...?
Gibt es...?
gipt es...?

...heating
...Heizung
hytsoong

...a fridge
...einen Kühlschrank
I-nen kewlshrank

...bedclothes
...Bettzeug
bet-tsoyg

...crockery
...Geschirr
gersheer

...cutlery
...Besteck
bershtek

...a washing machine
...eine Waschmaschine
I-ner vashmasheener

Is it fully equipped?
Ist es voll ausgestattet?
ist es fol owsgershtattet?

Is it electric or gas?
Ist es elektrisch oder Gas?
ist es elektrish ohder gas?

I need...
Ich brauche...
ish browkher...

...an electrician
...einen Elektriker
I-nen elektriker

...a plumber
...einen Klempner
I-nen klempner

...a gas man
...einen Heizungsfachmann
I-nen hytsoongz-fakhman

TRAVEL

ROAD

• Germany has an excellent transport system; the major cities are connected to one another and to the UK and USA by air. The clean and punctual trains of DB (Deutsche Bundesbahn – German Federal Railways) are part of a fully integrated transport network linking cities, towns and villages.

• Speed limits: motorways   no speed limit for cars,
                             except in busy areas
            built-up areas   50 km/h (30 mph)
            other roads   100 km/h (60 mph)

•Motorways: *Autobahnen* in Germany do not charge tolls, but a toll (*die Maut/die Gebühr*) is payable on some mountain roads and tunnels in Austria, and in Switzerland you must display a special sticker (*die Vignette*), available in Britain from the AA or RAC.

• Right of way: traffic coming from the right has priority at junctions, unless it's entering from, for example, a service road, or there is a priority sign (a yellow diamond, or an arrow in a triangle).

How do I get to (+ place name)/ to (+ building, street)...?	Wie komme ich nach/zu...? *vee kommer ish nakh/ tsoo...?*
How far is it to (+ place name)/ to (+ building, road)...?	Wie weit ist es nach/zu...? *vee vyt ist es nakh/ tsoo...?*
How long does it take?	Wie lange dauert es? *vee langer dowert es?*
Am I on the right road for...?	Bin ich auf der richtigen Straße nach...? *bin ish owf dair rishtigen shtraaser nakh...?*
Can you show it to me on the map/on the street map?	Können Sie es mir auf der Karte/auf dem Stadtplan zeigen? *kurnen zee es meer owf dair kaarter/ owf dem shtatplaan tsygen?*
Where can I park?	Wo kann ich parken? *vo kan ish parken?*

You may hear:

Nehmen Sie die Straße nach/über... *naimen zee dee shtraaser nakh/ewber...*	Take the road for/via...
Fahren Sie Richtung... *faaren zee rishtoong...*	Go in the direction of...

You should obtain a green card from your insurance company before taking your car abroad. Additional breakdown policies are also available. For full details contact the AA or RAC.

Sie sind auf der falschen Straße *zee zint owf dair falshen shtraaser*	You're on the wrong road
Sie müssen zurück nach… *zee mewssen tsoorewk nakh…*	You'll have to go back to…
nördlich/südlich von… *nurdlish/sewdlish fon…*	to the north/south of…
östlich/westlich von… *urstlish/vestlish fon…*	to the east/west of…
Fahren Sie… *faaren zee…*	Go…
…geradeaus *geraaderows*	…straight on
…nach links *nakh links*	…left
…nach rechts *nakh reshts*	…right
…bis zur ersten/zweiten Kreuzung *bis tsoor airsten/ tsvyten kroytsoong*	…to the first/ second junction
…bis zur Ampel *bis tsoor ampel*	…to the traffic lights

FILLING STATION/GARAGE

Where's the nearest filling station/garage?	Wo ist die nächste Tankstelle/ Reparaturwerkstatt? *vo ist dee neshste tank- shteller/reparatoor-verkshtat?*
Please fill the tank	Volltanken, bitte *foltanken, bitter*
lead-free	bleifrei/ unverbleit *blyfry/oonfairblyt*

diesel	Diesel
	deesel
Please check/change/repair	Bitte überprüfen/wechseln/ reparieren Sie ...
	bitter ewbrprewfen/veshseln/ repareeren zee ...
...the oil	...das Öl
	das url
...the water	...das Kühlwasser
	das kewlvasser
...the brake fluid	...die Bremsflüssigkeit
	dee brems-flewsigkyt
...the tyre	...den Reifen
	dain ryfen
...the spare tyre	...den Ersatzreifen
	dain erzats-ryfen
...the battery	...die Batterie
	dee bateree
...the bulb	...die Glühbirne
	dee glew-beerner
...the fanbelt	...den Keilriemen
	dain kylreemen
...the fuse	...die Sicherung
	dee zisheroong
...the spark plugs	...die Zündkerzen
	dee tsewnt-kairtsen
...the windscreen	...die Windschutzscheibe
	dee vintshoots-shyber
...the brakes	...die Bremsen
	dee bremzen
...the exhaust pipe	...den Auspuff
	dain owspoof

| ...the radiator | ...den Kühler |
| | *dain kewler* |

| Can you help me? | Können Sie mir helfen? |
| | *kurnun zee meer helfen?* |

| Do you do repairs? | Machen sie Reparaturen? |
| | *makhen zee reparatooren?* |

| The engine's running hot | Der Motor läuft heiß |
| | *dair motohr loyft hyss* |

BREAKDOWN

| Where's the nearest garage? | Wo ist die nächste Reparaturwerkstatt? |
| | *voh ist dee neshster reparatoor-vairkshtat?* |

| I've had a breakdown | Ich habe eine Panne |
| | *ish haaber I-ner panner* |

| I've got a flat tyre | Ich habe einen Platten |
| | *ish haaber I-nen platten* |

| I've run out of petrol | Mir ist das Benzin ausgegangen |
| | *meer ist das bentseen owsgergangen* |

| The engine won't start | Der Motor springt nicht an |
| | *dair motohr shpringt nisht an* |

| The engine is overheating | Der Motor läuft heiß |
| | *dair motohr loyft hyss* |

| The battery is flat | Die Batterie ist leer |
| | *dee bateree ist lair* |

| There's something wrong with the... | ...ist nicht in Ordnung |
| | *ist nisht in ordnoong* |

| Please send a mechanic/ a breakdown truck | Bitte schicken Sie einen Mechaniker/einen Abschleppwagen |
| | *bitter shikken zee I-nen mekaaniker/ I-nen abshlep-vaagen* |

I'm on the road from...to...	Ich bin auf der Straße zwischen...und... *ish bin owf dair shtraasser tsvishen...oont...*
I'm 5 kilometers from...	Ich bin fünf Kilometer von... *ish bin fewnf kilomaiter fon...*
How long will it take?	Wie lange dauert es? *vee langer dowert es?*

See page 156 for numbers.

ROAD TRAVEL

You may see:

Anliegerverkehr frei/ Nur für Anlieger	access to residents/ owners only
Ausfahrt	exit
Bahnübergang	railway crossing
Baustelle	roadworks
Durchgangsverkehr	through traffic
Einbahnstraße	one-way street
Einordnen	get in lane
Fahrradweg	cycle path
Fußgängerzone	pedestrian zone
Gefährliche Kurve	dangerous bend
Gegenverkehr	two-way traffic
Gesperrt für Fahrzeuge	closed to vehicles
Glatteis	black ice
Halteverbot	no stopping
Kriechspur	slow lane/crawler lane
Langsam fahren	slow

Most roadsigns are identical to those found in Britain. The words and phrases listed on this page are commonly found on roadsigns and notices.

Lkw	lorry/truck
Nicht überholen	no overtaking
Nur für Busse/Pkw	Buses/cars only
Parken nur mit Parkscheibe	Parking disc holders only
Parkplatz	car-park
Parkscheibe/Parkuhren	parking disc/parking meters
Pkw	car
Raststätte	services
Überholen verboten	no overtaking
Umleitung	diversion
…verboten	no…
Vorsicht	caution

BUYING TICKETS

When is the next train to Bonn?	Wann fährt der nächste Zug nach Bonn? *van fairt dair neshster tsoog nakh bon?*
When does it arrive?	Wann kommt er an? *van komt air an?*
Do I have to change?	Muss ich umsteigen? *moos ish oomshtygen?*
I'd like a … ticket to Bonn	Ich möchte eine Fahrkarte nach Bonn… *ish murshter I-ner faarkaarter nakh bon…*
…single (one way)	…einfach *I-nfakh*
…return	…hin und zurück *hin oont zoorewk*
…first class	…erster Klasse *airster klasser*

...second class	...zweiter Klasse *tsvyter klasser*
What does it cost?	Was kostet es? *vas kostet es?*
What about children?	Und für Kinder? *oont fewr kinnder?*
Are there reductions for children/students?	Gibt es Ermäßigungen für Kinder/Studenten? *gipt es airmaissigoongen* *fewr kinnder/shtoodenten?*
I'm a (non-)smoker	Ich bin (Nicht-)Raucher *ish bin (nisht-)rowkher*

BUYING TICKETS – AIR

Is it a direct flight?	Ist es ein Direktflug? *ist es I-n direktfloog?*
Is there a connection to Munich?	Gibt es einen Anschluss nach München? *gipt es I-nen an-shloos nakh* *mewnchen?*
When does the plane take off?	Wann ist der Abflug? *van ist dair abfloog?*
When do we land?	Wann landen wir? *van landen veer?*
What is the flight number?	Welche Flugnummer ist es? *velsher floog-noomer ist es?*
When must I check in?	Wann muss ich einchecken? *van moos ish I-ncheken?*
Is there an airport bus?	Gibt es einen Flughafenbus? *gipt es I-nen flooghaafen-boos?*
I'd like to...my reservation	Ich möchte meine Reservierung... *ish murshter myner* *rezerveeroong...*

...confirm	...bestätigen
	bershtaitigen
...alter	...umbuchen
	oombooken
...cancel	...annullieren
	anolleeren

You may see:

Abfahrt	Departures
Ankunft	Arrivals
Fluggäste/Passagiere	Passengers
Fluglinie	Airline
Gepäckausgabe	Luggage reclaim
Inland	Internal (flights)
Linienflug	Scheduled flight
Passkontrolle	Passport control
Zoll	Customs
Zollfreie Waren	Duty-free shop

RAIL

• The main types of train are:

TEE-Zug: Trans European Express (1st class only – supplement [*Zuschlag*] payable)

ICE: Inter City Express – first class supplement [*Zuschlag*] payable.

D-Zug: Express (supplement payable for journeys under 50km) (*Städteschnellzug* in Austria, *Schnellzug* in Austria, Switzerland)

E-Zug: Moderately fast train - does not stop at small stations.

N-Zug: Local train stopping at all stations (*Personenzug* in Austria, *Regionalzug* in Switzerland)

• Coaches on long-distance international trains are often regrouped along their route for different destinations. It is important to get on the right *Kurswagen* by checking the destination plate on the coaches; you can find the approximate position of the coach beforehand by looking at the *Wagenstandanzeiger* on the platform.

• Remember that German railways show two timetables:

> *Abfahrt* Departures   *Ankunft* Arrivals

• Other useful terms are:

> **Speisewagen** Dining car
>
> **Schlafwagen** Sleeping car with compartments containing a washbasin and one, two or three berths.
>
> **Liegewagen** Coach containing berths with sheets, blankets and pillows. Cheaper than the Schlafwagen.

• It is advisable to reserve your seat or berth in advance.

• German railway stations have luggage lockers where luggage may be left.

AT THE STATION

Where is/are the...?	Wo ist/sind...? *voh ist/zind...?*
...(currency) exchange office	...die Wechselstube *dee vehsel-shtoober*
...left-luggage counter (baggage check)	...die Gepäck- aufbewahrung *dee gerpeck- owfbervaaroong*
...lost property office	...das Fundbüro *das foont-bewroh*
...luggage check-in	...die Gepäckaufgabe *dee gerpeck-owfgaaber*
...luggage check-out	...die Gepäckausgabe *dee gerpeck-owsgaaber*

If you do not have time to buy a ticket before boarding the train, you may buy one from the guard (*Schaffner*) on the train, as long as you go and find him as soon as possible.

...news-stand	...das Zeitungskiosk *das tsytoongs-kee-osk*
...platform 2	...Gleis 2/Bahnsteig 2 *glys tsvy/baan-shtyg tsvy*
...reservations office	...die Platzreservierung *dee plats-reserveeroong*
...restaurant	...das Restaurant *das restaurong*
...snack bar	...der Schnellimbiss *dair shnel-imbis*
...ticket office/counter	...der Fahrkartenschalter *dair faar-kaarten-shalter*
...waiting room	...der Wartesaal *dair vaarter-zaal*
...the toilets	...die Toiletten *dee twaletten*
...luggage-lockers	...die Schließfächer *dee shlees-fesher*
...luggage-trolleys	...die Kofferkulis *dee koffer-kooliz*
I'd like to reserve...	Ich möchte...reservieren *ish murshter...rezerveeren*
...a seat/2 seats	...einen Platz/zwei Plätze *I-nen plats/tsvy pletser*
...by the window	...am Fenster *am fenster*
...in a no-smoking compartment	...in einem Nichtraucherabteil *in I-nem nisht-rowkherabtyl*
...in a smoking compartment	...in einem Raucherabteil *in I-nem rowkherabtyl*
...a berth in a sleeping car	...einen Platz im Schlafwagen *I-nen plats in shlaafvaagen*

Do I have to pay a surcharge?	Muss ich einen Zuschlag bezahlen?
	moos ish <u>I</u>-nen ts<u>oo</u>-shlaag berts<u>aa</u>len?
Will the train leave on time?	Fährt der Zug pünktlich ab?
	fairt dair tsoog p<u>e</u>wnktlish ap?
Will the train arrive on time?	Kommt der Zug pünktlich an?
	komt dair tsoog p<u>e</u>wnktlish an?
Is there enough time to change?	Reicht die Zeit zum Umsteigen?
	rysht dee tsyt tsoom <u>oo</u>mshtygen?
Does the train stop in Bonn?	Hält der Zug in Bonn?
	helt dair tsoog in bonn?
What platform does the train to Bonn leave from?	Auf welchem Gleis fährt der Zug nach Bonn ab?
	owf v<u>e</u>lshem glys fairt dair tsoog nakh bonn ap?
Does the train have a restaurant car/ sleeping car?	Führt der Zug einen Speisewagen/einen Schlafwagen?
	fewrt dair tsoog <u>I</u>-nen shp<u>y</u>zer-vaagen/<u>I</u>-nen shl<u>aa</u>f-vaagen?
Is this the train to Bonn?	Ist das der Zug nach Bonn?
	ist das dair tsoog nakh bonn?
I'd like to register (check) my luggage	Ich möchte mein Gepäck aufgeben
	ish m<u>u</u>rshter myn gerp<u>e</u>ck <u>ow</u>fgaiben

ON THE TRAIN

Is this seat free?	Ist dieser Platz frei?
	ist d<u>ee</u>zer plats fry?
This seat's taken	Dieser Platz ist besetzt
	d<u>ee</u>zer plats ist berz<u>e</u>tst

I think this is my seat	Ich glaube, das ist mein Platz *ish glowber, das ist myn plats*
I have a reservation for this seat	Ich habe eine Reservierung für diesen Platz *ish haaber I-ner resairveeroong fewr deezen plats.*
Excuse me. May I come past?	Entschuldigung. Kann ich bitte durch? *ent-shooldigoong, kan ish bitter doorsh?*
What's this place called?	Wie heißt dieser Ort? *vee hyst deezer ort?*
How long will the train stop here?	Wie lange hält der Zug hier? *vee langer helt dair tsoog heer?*
Where is my berth?	Wo ist meine Kabine? *voh ist myner kabeener?*
Please wake me at 6	Bitte wecken Sie mich um 6 Uhr *bitter veken zee mish um zekhs oor*
Would you bring me coffee at 6?	Würden Sie mir bitte um 6 Uhr Kaffee bringen? *vewrden zee meer bitter oom zekhs oor kafai bringen?*
Can you tell me when we get to...?	Sagen Sie mir bitte Bescheid, wenn wir in...ankommen...? *zaagen zee meer bitter bershyt ven veer in...ankommen...?*
Where are we?	Wo sind wir hier? *voh zint veer heer?*

You may hear:

Der nächste Zug nach Bonn fährt um... *dair neshster tsoog nakh bonn fairt oom...*	The next train to Bonn leaves at...

Steigen Sie in...um
shtygen zee in...oom

Change in...

Sie müssen einen Zuschlag
bezahlen
*zee mewssen I-nen tsooshlaag
bertsaalen*

You must pay a supplement

Der Fahrkartenschalter ist...
dair faarkartenshalter ist...

The ticket office is...

...da drüben
  da drewben

...over there

...links
  links

...on the left

...rechts
  reshts

...on the right

...oben
  ohben

...upstairs

...unten
  oonten

...downstairs

Der Zug hat...Minuten
Verspätung
*dair tsoog hat...minooten
fairshpaitoong*

The train will be...minutes late

Erste Klasse...des Zuges
airster klaser...des tsooges

First class...of the train

...an der Spitze...
  an dair shpitser...

...at the front...

...in der Mitte...
  in dair mitter...

...in the middle...

...am Ende...
  am ender...

...at the end...

You may see or hear:

(See also pages 65–67)

Achtung/Vorsicht! *akhtoong/fohrzisht*	Attention/watch out!
aussteigen *ows-shtygen*	to get off/out
einsteigen *I-nshtygen*	to get in/on
Nichtraucher *nisht-rowkher*	non-smoker
Notbremse *nohtbremzer*	emergency cord
planmäßig *plan-maisig*	scheduled
Platzkarte *plats-kaarter*	seat reservation
Raucher *rowkher*	smoker
sonn- und feiertags *zon oont fuertaagz*	Sundays and holidays
Strecke *shtreker*	route
umsteigen *oomshtygen*	to change
verkehrt nicht an… *fairkairt nisht an…*	does not run on…(days)
verkehrt nur an… *fairkairt noor an…*	runs only on…(days)
Zug fährt sofort ab! *tsoog fairt zofort ab!*	train now leaving!
zurücktreten! *tsoorewk-traiten!*	stand clear!

zuschlagpflichtig
tsooshlag-pflishtig

subject to supplementary
fare
(see note on page 52)

BUS, TRAM AND UNDERGROUND

• Local transport consists of buses, and in the larger cities,
trams, underground and the S-bahn (local rail/underground
network).

• Tickets, which may be used on any form of local transport,
vary in cost according to the number of zones crossed. Ticket
machines usually give change.

• In rural areas, rail links tie in with the bus services run by
DB (red) or the Post Office (yellow).

• Automatic ticket dispensers (*Fahrkartenautomat*) are wide-
spread. If you intend to make a number of journeys it may be
worth your while to buy a booklet of tickets.

I'd like a book of tickets	Ich möchte eine Sammelkarte *ish murshter I-ner zammel-kaarter*
Where is the...?	Wo ist...? *voh ist...?*
...bus stop	...die Haltestelle *dee halter-shtelle*
...bus station	...der Busbahnhof *dair boosbaanhof*
...underground station	...die U-Bahn-Station *dee oobaarn-statsyohn*
Does this bus stop in...?	Hält dieser Bus in...? *helt deezer boos in...?*
Can you tell me where to	Können Sie mir bitte

Tickets must usually be passed through an automatic stamping machine (*Entwerter*) as you get on the bus, tram or underground (subway).

	Bescheid
get off, please?	sagen, wo ich aussteigen muss? *kurnen zee meer bitter bershyt zaagen, voh ish ows-shtygen moos?*
I'd like to get off here	Ich möchte hier aussteigen *ish murshter ows-shtygen*
Does this bus go to...?	Fährt dieser Bus...? *fairt deezer boos...?*
Which bus goes to...?	Welcher Bus fährt...? *velsher boos fairt...?*
How often are the buses to...?	Wie oft fahren die Busse...? *vie oft faaren dee booser...?*
How many stops to...?	Wie viele Haltestellen sind es bis...? *veefeeler halter-shtellen zint es bis...?*
...the cathedral	...zum Dom *tsoom dohm*
...the museum	...zum Museum *tsoom moozai-oom*
...the Old Town	...zur Altstadt *tsoor alt-shtat*
...the theatre	...zum Theater *tsoom tai-aater*
...the youth hostel	...zur Jugendherberge *tsoor Yoogenthairbairger*
...Würzburg	...nach Würzburg *nakh vewrtsboorg*
When is the next bus to...?	Wann fährt der nächste Bus nach...? *van fairt dair neshster boos nakh...?*

How much is the fare to...?	Was kostet es nach...?
	vas kostet es nakh...?

You may hear:

Nehmen Sie Bus Linie 6	Take a number 6
naimen zee boos leenyer zekhs	
Ein Bus fährt alle 10 Minuten	A bus leaves every 10 minutes
I-n boos fairt aller tsain minooten	

You may see:

Bushaltestelle	regular bus stop
Bedarfshaltestelle	stops on request

BOATS AND FERRIES

When is there a boat for...?	Wann fährt ein Schiff nach...?
	van fairt I-n shif nakh...?
Where does it leave from?	Wo fährt es ab?
	voh fairt es ap?
When do we call in...?	Wann legen wir in...an?
	van laigen veer in...an?
How long does the crossing last?	Wie lange dauert die Überfahrt?
	vee langer dowert dee ewberfaart?
We'd like a trip on the river	Wir möchten eine Flussfahrt machen
	veer murshten I-ner floos-faart makhen
We'd like a cabin	Wir möchten eine Kabine
	veer murshten I-ner kabeener
There's...	Wir sind...
	veer zint...
...1 adult/2 adults	...ein Erwachsener/zwei Erwachsene
	I-n airvakhsener/tsvy airvakhsener

Look for the sign *Taxistand* (taxi rank). It is not usual to hail a taxi.
Tipping: about 10%.

...1 child/2 chidren	...ein Kind/zwei Kinder
	I-n kint/tsvy kinnder
We have...	Wir haben...
	veer haaben…
...a car	...ein Auto
	I-n owtoh
...bicycles	...Fahrräder
	faar-raider
...a caravan	...einen Wohnwagen
	I-nen vohn-vaagen
...a motorbike	...ein Motorrad
	I-n motohr-raat

TAXI

Where can I get a taxi?	Wo finde ich ein Taxi?
	voh finder ish I-n taxi?
Please get me a taxi	Können Sie mir bitte ein Taxi rufen?
	kurnen zee meer bitter I-n taxi roofen?
Please take me to...	Fahren Sie mich bitte...
	faaren zee mish bitter…
...this address	...zu dieser Adresse
	tsoo deezer addresser
...the station	...zum Bahnhof
	tsoom baanhohf
...the airport	...zum Flughafen
	tsoom flooghaafen
Could you help me with my luggage?	Können Sie mir mit meinem Gepäck helfen?
	kurnen zee meer mit mynem gerpeck helfen?
Please stop here	Bitte halten Sie hier
	bitter halten zee heer

Wait for me, please	Bitte warten Sie auf mich *bitter vaarten zee owf mish*
How much is it?	Was kostet es? *vas kostet es?*
Keep the change	Es stimmt so *es shtimmt zoh*
Can you give me a receipt?	Können Sie mir bitte eine Quittung geben? *kurnen zee meer bitter I-ner kvitoong gaiben?*

CAR HIRE

I'd like to hire a car	Ich möchte ein Auto mieten *ish murshter I-n owtoh meeten*
I'd like a small/medium/ large one	Ich möchte ein kleines/ eine mittelgroßes/ ein großes *ish murshter I-n klynes/ I-n mittelgrohses/ I-n grohses*
I'd like it for...	Ich möchte es für... *ish murshter es fewr...*
...a day	...einen Tag *I-nen taag*
...2 days	...zwei Tage *tsvy taager*
...a week	...eine Woche *I-ner vokher*
What are the tariffs per day/week?	Was sind die Tarife pro Tag/pro Woche? *vas zint dee tareefer proh taag/proh vokher?*

Look for the sign *Autoverleih* or *Autovermietung.*

Can I leave the car in…?	Kann ich das Auto in … zurück-geben?
	kan ish das <u>ow</u>toh in … tsoor<u>ewk</u>-gaiben?
I'd like comprehensive insurance	Ich möchte eine Vollkaskoversicherung
	ish m<u>ur</u>shter <u>I</u>-ner folkaskoh-fairzisheroong
How much deposit must I pay?	Wie viel muss ich hinterlegen?
	veefeel moos ish hinterl<u>aig</u>en?
Here is my driving licence/ my passport	Hier ist mein Führerschein/ mein Pass
	heer ist myn <u>few</u>rershyn/myn pass

You may see:

Abfahrt	Departures
Abflug	Departures (airport)
Ankunft	Arrivals
Ausgang	Exit
Auskunft	Information
Ausland	abroad
Bahnhofspolizei	railway police
Behinderte	disabled
besetzt	occupied
bezahlen	pay
Damen	ladies
Eingang	Entrance
Einstieg nur mit Fahrausweis	buy ticket before boarding
Einstieg vorn/hinten	board at front/rear
einwerfen	insert
entwerten	stamp, validate (ticket)

Erwachsene	adult
Fahrausweis/Fahrkarte/Fahrschein	ticket
Fahrgäste	passengers
Fahrplan	timetable
Familienkarte	family ticket
Flughafenbus	airport bus
Flugplan	flight schedule
Flugsteig	gate
frei	free
Geldeinwurf	insert money here
Geldrückgabe	returned coins
Gepäckschließfächer	luggage lockers
Gleis	platform
Gruppenkarte	group ticket
Hafen	port, harbour
Haltestelle	bus/tram stop
Hauptbahnhof (Hbf)	Main station
Herren	men
Imbiss	snack (-bar)
Inland	domestic
kein Ausstieg/Einstieg	no exit/entry
kein Zugang	no entry
Kinder	children
Kurswagen	Through coach
Mehrfahrtenkarte	multi-journey ticket
Minigruppenkarte	group ticket (4 people)
Monatskarte	monthly card
Münzen	coins

Netz	network
Nichtraucher	Non-smoker (compartment)
nicht hinauslehnen	do not lean out
Notausgang	emergency exit
nur werktags	weekdays only
Raucher	Smoker (compartment)
Reiseauskunft	travel information
samstags	Saturdays
S-Bahn	local railway network
Senioren	senior citizens
sonn -und feiertags	Sundays and public holidays
Strecke	route
Tageskarte	day ticket
U-Bahn	tube, underground
Wagenstandanzeiger	Order of carriages (see introductory note on page 53)
Wartesaal	waiting room
zu den Gleisen/Zügen	to the platforms/trains
zuschlagflichtig	supplement payable

SIGHTSEEING

Where's the information office?

Wo ist das Informationsbüro?
voh ist das informatsyohns-bewroh?

What are the main places of interest?

Was sind die Hauptsehens-würdigkeiten?
vas zint dee howpt-zaiens-vewrdikh-kyten?

What is there of interest to children?

Was ist für Kinder interessant?
vas ist fewr kinnder interessant?

Do you have a street map?	Haben sie einen Stadtplan? *h<u>aa</u>bun zee <u>I</u>-nen sht<u>a</u>t-plaan?*
Is it easy to get there on foot?	Kann man das leicht zu Fuss erreichen? *kan man das lysht tsoo fooss air<u>y</u>shen?*
Where is/are the...?	Wo ist/sind...? *voh ist/zint...?*
...art gallery	...die Kunstgalerie *dee k<u>oo</u>nstgalleree*
...castle	...das Schloss/die Burg *das shlos/dee boorg*
...cathedral	...die Kathedrale/der Dom *dee katedr<u>aa</u>ler/dair d<u>o</u>hm*
...church	...die Kirche *dee k<u>ee</u>rsher*
...concert hall	...die Konzerthalle *dee konts<u>air</u>t-haller*
...conference centre	...die Kongresshalle *dee kongr<u>e</u>ss-haller*
...exhibition centre	...das Messegelände *das m<u>e</u>sser-gerlender*
...market place	...der Marktplatz *dair m<u>aa</u>rkt-plats*
...museum	...das Museum *das mooz<u>ai</u>-um*
...shopping centre	...das Einkaufszentrum *das <u>I</u>-nkowfs-tsentroom*
...sports centre	...das Sportzentrum *das shp<u>o</u>rt-tsentroom*

Most towns have a tourist information office, signposted with a large letter 'i'. They can help with information not only about places of interest and events, but also booking accommodation.

Most musems, galleries and places of interest in Germany are closed on Mondays.

...town centre	...die Innenstadt
	dee innen-shtat
Is the...worth visiting?	Ist...sehenswert?
	ist...zai-enzvairt?
Have we got time to visit...?	Haben wir noch Zeit, ...zu besichtigen?
	haaben veer nokh tsyt, ...tsoo berzikhtigen?
I'm interested in...	Ich interessiere mich für...
	ish interesseerer mish fewr...
...archaeology	...Archäologie
	arsh-eh-ologee
...art	...Kunst
	koonst
...history	...Geschichte
	ger-shishter
...music	...Musik
	moozeek
...natural history	...Naturkunde
	natoor-koonder
...technology	...Technik
	teshnik

ADMISSION

Is it open on Saturdays/today/tomorrow?	Ist es samstags/heute/morgen geöffnet?
	ist es zamztaagz/hoyter/morgen ger-urfnet?
What are the opening times?	Was sind die Öffnungszeiten?
	vas zint dee urfnoongz-tsyten?
There are four of us	Wir sind 4 Personen
	veer zint feer pairzohnen

2 adults/children	2 Erwachsene/Kinder *tsvy airvakhsener/kinnder*
I'd like a guide book (in English)	Ich möchte einen Reiseführer (auf Englisch) *ish murshter I-nen ryzer-fewrer* *(owf ennglish)*
When does it close?	Wann schließt es? *van shleest es?*
How much does it cost to go in?	Was kostest der Eintritt? *vas kostest dair I-ntritt?*
Is it suitable for disabled people?	Ist es behindertengerecht? *ist es berhinderten-geresht?*
Is there wheelchair access?	Kann man mit einem Rollstuhl hinein? *kan man mit I-nen rol-shtool hin-In?*
Can I take photographs?	Darf man fotografieren? *darf man fohtografeeren?*
Are there special rates for...?	Gibt es Ermäßigungen für...? *gipt es air-maissigoongen fewr...?*
...children	...Kinder *kinnder*
...disabled people	...Behinderte *ber-hinnderter*
...groups	...Gruppen *groopen*
...pensioners/senior citizens	...Rentner/Senioren *rentner/zeniohren*
....students	...Studenten *shtoodenten*

You may see:

Eintrittspreise	Admission charges
Eintritt frei	Admission free
Fotografieren verboten Fotografieren nicht gestattet }	No photography
Rauchen verboten	No smoking

IN THE COUNTRY

• The countryside and forests are crisscrossed with large numbers of well-marked footpaths (*Wanderwege*). A map showing the footpaths in the locality (*eine Wanderkarte*) will help you get the best out of these.

How far is it to...?	Wie weit ist es nach...? *vee vyt ist es nakh...?*
How long will it take?	Wie lange dauert es? *vee langer dowert es?*
How do I get to...?	Wie komme ich nach...? *vee kommer ish nakh...?*
Is there a pub near here?	Ist ein Gasthaus in der Nähe? *ist I-n gast-hous in dair naier?*
Where does this footpath/ road lead to?	Wohin führt dieser Fußweg/diese Straße? *voh-hin fewrt deezer foossvaig/deezer shtraasser?*
What's the name of this...?	Wie heißt...? *vee hysst...?*
...castle	...das Schloss *das shloss*
...lake	...der See *dair zai*

In the mountain areas, signposts show distances in hours rather than kilometres.

...river	...der Fluss *dair flooss*
...village	...das Dorf *das dorf*
What's that called in German?	Wie heißt das auf Deutsch? *vee hysst das owf doych?*

DESCRIBING THINGS AND PLACES

It's...	Es ist... *es ist...*
...amazing	...erstaunlich *air-shtownlish*
...awful	...schrecklich *shreklish*
...beautiful	...schön *shurn*
...boring	...langweilig *langvylig*
...depressing	...deprimierend *deprimeerent*
...impressive	...beeindruckend *ber-I-ndrookent*
...interesting	...interessant *interessant*
...lovely	...wunderschön *voondershurn*
...picturesque	...malerisch *maalerish*
...pretty	...hübsch *hewpsh*
...romantic	...romantisch *rohmantish*

...strange

...ugly

I (don't) like it

...seltsam
zeltzaam

...hässlich
hesslish

Es gefällt mir (nicht)
es gerfelt meer (nisht)

EATING OUT

• There is a special **What's on the menu?** section listing items of food and German specialities on page 88.

• It is possible to buy a meal at any time of day, and well into the evening, in Germany, Austria and Switzerland. You will find foreign restaurants (particularly Italian) and fast-food cafeterias as well as the usual cafés and pubs where you can eat *gut bürgerlich* (good home-cooking).

• Each area has its own specialities of dishes, breads, cakes, sausages, and beers or wines.

In all but fast-food shops and snack- bars, there will be waiters or waitresses. German law allows children and young people to buy alcohol (but not spirits) at 14 if accompanied by an adult, 16 if not. Children are allowed in pubs.

PLACES TO EAT AND DRINK

Brauhaus/ Bierstube Rather like a pub or tavern. The emphasis is on beer rather than food.

Café/ Café-Konditorei Coffee shop. The cheapest are self-service cafés where the customers stand at small high tables. Cafés are often linked to a *Konditorei*, a cake/pastry shop. If you want a slice of cake with your drink, make your selection out in the shop (unless you know the name of what you want); you will be given a piece of paper (*ein Zettel*) which you give to the waitress when you place your drinks order.

Gasthaus/ Gasthof Inn; found in the country or in small towns, with snacks, full meals and drinks on offer.

Gaststätte Restaurant.

Kaffeehaus Café, in Austria.

Raststätte/ Rasthof Motorway services and restaurant.

Ratskeller/ Ratstube Café or restaurant near to, or in the cellar of the town hall.

Schnellimbiss/ Imbiss Snack bar, selling mainly beer and sausages.

Weinstube Rather like a Gasthof; found in wine-producing areas.

You may see:

Heute Ruhetag	Closed today
Montag Betriebsruhe	Closed on Mondays
Durchgehend warme Küche	Hot meals available all day
Straßenverkauf Zum Mitnehmen }	Take away
Reserviert	Reserved
Stammtisch	Table reserved for landlord and regulars (in pubs)

Meals

Breakfast *(das Frühstück)*: a fairly substantial meal of bread, rolls, cheese, cold meats and sausages, and jam, accompanied by coffee, tea, milk, and/ or fruit juice.

Lunch *(das Mittagessen)*: this is often the main meal of the day, and is usually accompanied by salads. It is often not followed by a pudding.

Evening meal *(das Abendessen)*: when taken at home, it is often rather like breakfast; when guests are invited, or in restaurants, a cooked meal is more normal.

Afternoon tea *(Kaffee und Kuchen)*: this is often taken at weekends, and usually consists of coffee and various cakes/ pastries.

RESERVATIONS

Have you got a table free?	Haben Sie einen Tisch frei? *haaben zee I-nen tish fry?*
I'd like to reserve a table for 4	Ich möchte einen Tisch für vier reservieren *ish murshter I-nen tish fewr feer rezerveeren*
We're coming at 9	Wir kommen um neun *veer kommen oom noyn*
We'd like a table...	Wir möchten einen Tisch... *veer murshten I-nen tish...*
...by the window	...am Fenster *am fenster*
...in a no-smoking area	...in der Nichtraucherecke *in dair nisht-rowkher-eker*
...outside	...im Freien *im fryen*

Don't sit at a table marked *Stammtisch* – it's reserved for a particular group of regular customers.

When ordering a meal in an inn it is worth bearing in mind that the main courses are substantial; a starter and a pudding are often unnecessary, unless you're very hungry.

...on the terrace	...auf der Terrasse
	owf dair tairasser
My name is...	Ich heiße...
	ish hysser...
Can I pay by credit card?	Kann ich mit Kreditkarte bezahlen?
	kan ish mit kredeetkarter bertsaalen?
I have a reservation	Ich habe reserviert
	ish haaber resairveert

ORDERING

Waiter/ Waitress	Herr Ober/Bedienung!
	hair ohber/berdeenoong!
May I have the menu, please?	Kann ich die Speisekarte haben, bitte?
	kan ish dee shpyzer-kaarter haaben, bitter?
May we have the wine list, please?	Können wir die Weinkarte haben, bitte?
	kurnen veer dee vynkaarter haaben, bitter?
I'm/ We're ready to order now	Ich möchte/Wir möchten jetzt bestellen
	ish murshter/veer murshten yetst bershtellen
I/ We haven't decided yet	Ich bin/Wir sind noch nicht so weit
	ish bin/veer zint nokh nisht zoh vyt
I/ We'll order something to drink first	Ich bestelle/Wir bestellen zuerst etwas zu trinken
	ish bershtelle/veer bershtellen tsooairst etvas tsoo trinken

Do you have any...?	Haben Sie...?
	haaben zee...?
I'd just like a snack	Ich möchte nur eine Kleinigkeit essen
	ish murshter noor I-ner klynigkyt essen
What do you recommend?	Was empfehlen Sie?
	vas empfailen zee?
Do you have any local dishes?	Haben Sie Gerichte aus der Gegend?
	haaben zee gerishter ows dair gaigent?
What is that?	Was ist das?
	vas ist das?
Is salad/ vegetables included?	Ist das mit Salat/Gemüse?
	ist das mit zalaat/germewser?
Do you have a children's menu?	Haben Sie einen Kinderteller?
	haaben zee I-nen kinnderteller?
Do you have any vegetarian dishes?	Haben Sie vegetarische Gerichte?
	haaben zee vegetaarisher gerishter?
I'd like my steak ...	Ich möchte mein Steak ...
	ish murshter myn shtaik...
...rare	blutig
	blootig
...medium	halbdurch
	halp-doorsh
...well done	durchgebraten
	doorsh-geerbraaten
I'm not allowed to eat...	Ich darf...nicht essen
	ish daarf...nisht essen
...eggs	...Eier
	I-er

...fat	...Fett *fet*
...flour	...Mehl *mail*
...sugar	....Zucker *tsooker*
...nuts	...Nüsse *newsser*
We'd all/ both like	Wir möchten alle/beide... *veer murshten aler/ byder...*
I'd like the menu at 30 Euros/ the dish of the day	Ich hätte gern das Menü zu dreißig Euro/das Tagesgericht *ish hetter gairn das menew tsoo drysig oyroh/das taagesgerisht*
That's for him/ her/ me	Das ist für ihn/sie/mich *das ist fewr een/zee/ mish*
The same for me, please	Das gleiche für mich, bitte *das glykher fewr mish bitter*
Could I have...instead?	Kann ich statt dessen...haben? *kan ish shtat dessen...haaben?*
Please may I have...?	Kann ich bitte...haben? *kan ish bitter...haaben?*
...some more	...etwas mehr *etvas mair*
...some (more) bread	...(noch) etwas Brot *(nokh) etvas broht*
...some (more) butter	...(noch) etwas Butter *(nokh) etvas booter*
...a (-nother) pot of coffee	...(noch) ein Kännchen Kaffee *(nokh) I-n kenshen kafai*
...a (-nother) cup of tea	...(noch) eine Tasse Tee *(nokh) I-ner tasser tai*
...a (-nother) glass of wine	...(noch) ein Glas Wein *(nokh) I-n glaas vyn*

...a (-nother) portion of...	...(noch) eine Portion... *(nokh) I-ner portsiohn...*
No more, thank you	Nichts mehr, danke *nishts mair, danker*

PROBLEMS & QUERIES

I ordered...	Ich habe...bestellt *ish haaber...bershtelt*
We've been waiting for 20 minutes	Wir warten schon seit zwanzig Minuten *veer vaarten shohn zyt tsvantsig minooten*
May I have a (-nother)...	Kann ich...haben? *kan ish...haaben?*
...fork	...eine (andere) Gabel *I-ner (anderer) gaabel*
...glass	...ein (anderes) Glas *I-n (anderes) glaas*
...knife	...ein (anderes) Messer *I-n (anderes) messer*
...spoon	...einen (anderen) Löffel... *I-nen (anderen) lurfel*
...plate	...einen Teller *I-nen teller*
This isn't clean	Das ist nicht sauber *das ist nisht zowber*
This is...	Das ist... *das ist...*
...burnt	...angebrannt *angerbrant*
...cold	...kalt *kalt*
...not fresh	...nicht frisch *nisht frisch*

...overcooked
...verkocht
fairkokht

...too salty/ sweet
...zu salzig/süß
tsoo zaltsig/zewss

...underdone
...nicht gar
nisht gaar

PAYING THE BILL

I'd like to pay, please
Ich möchte zahlen, bitte
ish murshter tsaalen, bitter

We're paying together/ separately
Wir bezahlen zusammen/ getrennt
veer bertsaalen tsoozammen/ gertrent

There seems to be a mistake in the bill
Ich glaube, Sie haben sich verrechnet
ish glowber, zee haaben zish fairekhnet

What is this amount for?
Wofür steht dieser Betrag?
vohfewr stait deezer bertraag?

Does that include service?
Ist das mit Bedienung?
ist das mit berdeenoong?

Do you accept traveller's cheques/ credit cards?
Nehmen Sie Reiseschecks/ Kreditkarten?
naimen zee ryzer-sheks/ kredeet-kaarten?

I don't have enough cash
Ich habe nicht genug in bar
ish haaber nisht gernoog in baar

You've given me the wrong change
Sie haben mir falsch herausgegeben
zee haaben meer falsch hairowsgergaiben

| Keep the change | Stimmt so
shtimmt so |
| May I have a receipt? | Kann ich eine Quittung haben bitte?
kan ish <u>I</u>-ner kv<u>i</u>ttoong h<u>aa</u>ben b<u>i</u>tter? |

You may hear

Bitte schön?
b<u>i</u>tter shurn?

Was darf es sein?
vas darf es zyn?

Was möchten Sie?
vas m<u>u</u>rshten zee?

} What would you like?

Haben Sie schon gewählt?
h<u>aa</u>ben zee shohn gerv<u>ai</u>lt?

Haben Sie etwas ausgesucht?
h<u>aa</u>ben zee <u>e</u>tvas <u>aw</u>sgezookht?

} Have you decided yet?

Sonst noch etwas?
zonst nokh <u>e</u>tvas?

Anything else?

...haben wir nicht mehr
  h<u>aa</u>ben veer nisht mair

We haven't any more...

Möchten Sie einen Nachtisch?
m<u>u</u>rshten zee <u>I</u>-nen n<u>a</u>kh-tish?

Would you like a dessert?

Guten Appetit!
g<u>oo</u>ten appet<u>ee</u>t!

Enjoy your meal!

Hat es Ihnen geschmeckt?
hat ess <u>ee</u>nen gershm<u>e</u>ckt?

Did you enjoy that?

You may see:

Hauptgerichte	main courses
hausgemacht	home-made
Imbisse	snacks

Im Preis inbegriffen	included in the price
Inklusive Bedienung und Mehrwertsteuer	service and VAT included
Mit Beilage	with salad or vegetables
Nachspeisen	desserts
Nur auf Bestellung	to order only
Spezialität des Hauses	speciality of the house
Tagesgedeck/Tagesmenü	set menu of the day
Tagesgericht	dish of the day

NON-ALCOHOLIC DRINKS

I'd like a/an...	Ich möchte...
	ish murshter...
...apple juice	...einen Apfelsaft
	I-nen apfelzaft
...blackcurrant juice	...einen Johannisbeersaft
	I-nen Yohanisbairzaft
...chocolate	...eine Schokolade
	I-ner shokolaader
...coffee	...einen Kaffee
	I-nen kafai
...Coke	...eine Cola
	I-ner kohla
...fruit juice	...einen Fruchtsaft
	I-nen frookhtzaft
...lemonade	...eine Limonade
	I-ner limonaader
...fizzy/ still mineral water	...ein Mineralwasser mit/ohne Kohlensäure
	I-n mineraalvasser mit/ohner kohlenzoyrer
...orange juice	...einen Orangensaft
	I-nen oranjenzaft

...tea	...einen Tee
	I-nen tai
...herb tea	...einen Kräutertee
	I-nen kroytertai
...tomato juice	...einen Tomatensaft
	I-nen tomaatenzaft
...tonic water	...ein Tonic
	I-n tonik
a cup	eine Tasse
	I-ner tasser
a pot (holds about 2 cups)	ein Kännchen
	I-n kenshen
a black coffee	einen schwarzen Kaffee
	I-nen shvaartsen kafai
with cream	mit Sahne
	mit zaaner
with milk	mit Milch
	mit milsh
decaffeinated	koffeinfrei
	koffe-eenfry
espresso	einen Espresso
	I-nen espressoh
with lemon	mit Zitrone
	mit tsitrohner

BEER

I'd like...	Ich möchte...
	ish murshter
...a glass of...	...ein Glas...
	I-n glaas...
...two glasses of...	...zwei Glas...
	tsvy glaas...
...a bottle of...	...eine Flasche...
	I-ner flasher...

Tea is served without milk unless requested.

...two bottles of...

...zwei Flaschen...
*tsvy fl*a*shen...*

...a tankard (litre)...

...eine Maß...
I-ner maas...

...another beer, please

...noch ein Bier, bitte
*nokh I-n beer b*i*tter*

You may hear:

Altbier *a*l*tbeer*	a top-fermented, dark beer
Bier *beer*	beer
Bockbier/ Doppelbock *b*o*kbeer/ d*o*ppelbok*	[types of] strong beer
Ein Dunkles *I-n d*oo*nkles*	a dark beer
Ein Helles *I-n h*e*lles*	a light-coloured beer
Malzbier *m*a*ltsbeer*	dark, sweet, low in alcohol
Märzen *m*ai*rtsen*	a strong, light beer
Pils/ Pilsner *pils/ p*i*lsner*	like lager – the most common type of beer
...vom Fass *fom fass*	draught
Weißbier/ Weizenbier *v*y*sbeer/ v*y*tsenbeer*	a pale, fizzy beer made from wheat

Almost every town in Germany has its brewery, and there are dozens of types of beer, some brewed only at particular times of the year.

WINE

• Germany, Austria and Switzerland all produce wine. If you are in or near a wine-producing region, all pubs and restaurants will stock locally-produced wines, although you may be able to buy wines from other parts of Europe too.

The flabby, over-sweetened *Liebfraumilch* and *Hock* which are often the only German wines available in most British supermarkets and off-licences are unknown in Germany.

I'd like...	Ich möchte...
	ish murshter
... a glass of...	...ein Glas...
	I-n glaas...
...a bottle of...	...eine Flasche...
	I-ner flasher...
...red wine	...Rotwein
	rohtvyn
...white wine	...Weißwein
	vysvyn
...rosé	...Rosé
	rohzay
...sparkling wine/ champagne	...Sekt
	zekt
...white wine with soda/ mineral water	...eine Schorle
	I-ner shorler

QUALITY AND FLAVOUR

crisp	frisch/ herb
	frish/ hairp
dry	trocken
	trocken
fruity	fruchtig
	frookhtig

In pubs, the waiter or waitress will often mark your beermat each time you order a drink – you pay at the end of the evening. Almost all pubs have a waiter service, and it is normal to drink sitting down. No-one stands at the bar.

You could also try *Schillerwein*, which is made by fermenting white and red grapes together, or *Weißherbst*, which is a very light wine made from bluish-skinned grapes.

sweet	süß	
	zewss	
light	leicht	
	lysht	
full-bodied	vollmundig	
	follmoondig	
table-wine/ 'plonk'	Tafelwein	
	taafelvyn	

• The phrase 'Aus den Ländern der EU' may be included on the label. This indicates that most of the contents of the bottle are from other European countries; these wines are usually of very poor quality.

QbA *koo bai aa*	(Qualitätswein aus den bestimmten Anbaugebieten)	a blended wine from a certified region e.g. Mosel, Rhein
QmP *koo em pai*	(Qualitätswein mit Prädikat)	a quality wine with a title
	Kabinett *kabinett*	high quality
	Spätlese *shpaitlaizer*	late vintage
	Auslese *owslaizer*	late vintage from specially selected grapes
	Beerenauslese *bairen-owslaizer*	made from selected over-ripe grapes
	Trockenbeerenauslese *trokenbairen-owslaizer*	made from grapes so over-ripe they are like raisins.
	Eiswein *I-svyn*	an intense wine made from frozen grapes

• The QmP titles indicate stages, not of increasing quality, but of increasing intensity and, usually, sweetness. With most savoury foods, a *Kabinett* or dry *(trocken) Spätlese* is recommended.

• A *Qualitätswein* (quality wine) will also have the name of the village and the vineyard where it was produced:

e.g. *Eltviller Langenstück – Eltville* is the village, *Langenstück* is the vineyard.

MAIN GRAPE VARIETIES

<u>White wines</u>

Riesling *reezling*	fresh; older wines elegant
Silvaner *zilvaaner*	gentle flavour
Müller-Thurgau *mewler-toorgow*	fruity, rounded
Gewürztraminer *gervewrts-trameener*	tending to spicy flavour

<u>Red wines</u>

Spätburgunder *shpaitboorgoonder*	the *pinot noir*; can be quite full-bodied in a good year
Lemberger *lembairger*	can be dry, full-bodied, but varies according to vineyard (SW Germany only)
Portugieser *portoogeezer*	rounded flavour
Trollinger *trolinger*	fresh and fruity (SW Germany only)

OTHER ALCOHOLIC DRINKS

I'd like a/ an/ some…	Ich möchte… *ish murshter…*
…brandy	…einen Weinbrand *I-nen vynbrant*

...cider	...einen Apfelwein/ Apfelmost
	I-nen apfelvyn/ apfel-mosst
...cognac	...einen Kognak
	I-nen konyak
...gin	...einen Gin
	I-nen jin

• **Doornkaat** *(doornkaat)* and **Steinhäger** *(shtynhaiger)* are the two best-known varieties of *Schnapps*.

...liqueur	...einen Likör
	I-nen likur
...port	...einen Portwein
	I-nen portvyn
...rum	...einen Rum
	I-nen room
...sherry	...einen Sherry
	I-nen sherri
...vermouth	...einen Wermut
	I-nen vairmut
...vodka	...einen Wodka
	I-nen vodka
...whisky	...einen Whisky
	I-nen viskee
neat (straight)	pur
	poor
with ice (on the rocks)	mit Eis
	mit I-s

WHAT'S ON THE MENU?

The immense variety of German regional cookery makes it impossible to do much more here than to list the main vocabulary to be found on menus. Most menus explain what goes into each dish.

German specialities include *Geist* (a clear spirit made from fruit e.g. *Kirschgeist* is the cherry variety), *Korn* (corn brandy) and *Schnapps* (a strong, clear brandy).

Ananas	*ananas*	pineapple
Apfel	*apfel*	apple
Apfelsine	*apfelzeener*	orange
Aprikose	*aprikohze*	apricot
Artischocken	*aartishohken*	artichokes
Auberginen	*ohberjeenen*	aubergines
Auflauf	*owflowf*	casserole
Austern	*owstern*	oysters
Back-	*bak-*	roasted, baked
Backpflaumen	*bak-pflowmen*	prunes
Baiser	*bezai*	meringue
Banane	*banaaner*	banana
Bauernfrühstück	*bowern-frewstewck*	potato and bacon omelette
Bedienung	*berdeenoong*	service
Beilagen	*by-laagen*	side-dish (vegetable or salad)
Berliner	*berleener*	jam doughnut
Birne	*beerner*	pear
Blumenkohl	*bloomen-kohl*	cauliflower
Blutwurst	*bloot-voorst*	black pudding
Bockwurst	*bokvoorst*	frankfurter
Bohnen	*bohnen*	beans
grüne	*grewner*	green (French)
weiße	*vysser*	white (haricot)
Brat-	*braat*	roasted
Braten	*braaten*	roast meat

Bratwurst	_br**aa**tvoorst_	fried sausage
Brokkoli	_br**o**kolee_	broccoli
Brombeeren	_br**o**mbeeren_	blackberries
Brot	_broht_	bread
Brötchen	_br**u**rtshen_	bread roll
Champignons	_sh**a**mpinyongs_	mushrooms
Currywurst	_c**u**rry-voorst_	sausage with curry sauce
Datteln	_d**a**tteln_	dates
Dorsch	_dorsh_	cod
Eier	_**I**-er_	eggs
mit Einlage	_mit **I**-nlaager_	egg, vegetables, etc. added to a clear soup
Eintopf	_**I**-ntopf_	stew
Eisbecher	_**I**-sbesher_	sundae/ice cream
englisch	_**e**nnglish_	rare (meat)
Ente	_**e**nter_	duck
Erbsen	_**ai**rbzen_	peas
Erdbeeren	_**ai**rdbairen_	strawberries
Erdnüsse	_**ai**rdnewsser_	peanuts
Essig	_**e**ssig_	vinegar
Feigen	_f**u**gen_	figs
Feldsalat	_f**e**lt-salaat_	lamb's lettuce
Fenchel	_f**e**nshel_	fennel
Filet	_fil**ai**_	fillet
Fisch	_fish_	fish

Fleischkäse	*flysh-kaiser*	meat loaf
Fleischpastete	*flysh-pastaiter*	pâté
Forelle	*foreller*	trout
Frikadelle	*frickadeller*	meat rissole
Frühlingsrolle	*frewlings-roller*	spring roll
Gans	*gans*	goose
Garnelen	*gaarnailen*	prawns
garniert	*gaarneert*	garnished
Gebäck	*gerbek*	cakes/pastries/biscuits
gebacken	*gerbaken*	baked
gemischter Salat	*germishter zalaat*	mixed salad
Gemüse	*germewser*	vegetables
geräuchert	*geroyshert*	smoked
gebraten	*gerbraaten*	roasted
gedämpft	*gerdempft*	steamed
Geflügel	*gerflewgel*	poultry
gefüllt	*gerfewlt*	stuffed
gegrillt	*gergrillt*	grilled
gehackt	*gerhakt*	chopped/minced
gekocht	*gerkokht*	cooked/boiled
Getränke	*gertrenker*	drinks
gewürzt	*gervewrtst*	flavoured with spices
Grießklößchen	*grees-klursshen*	semolina dumplings
grüner Salat	*grewner zalaat*	green salad
Gurken	*goorken*	cucumbers/gherkins

Hackfleisch	*hakflysh*	minced meat
Hähnchen	*hainshen*	chicken
Haselnüsse	*haazelnewsser*	hazelnuts
Hauptgerichte	*howpt-gerishter*	main courses
Hauptspeisen	*howpt-spyzern*	main courses
hausgemacht	*hows-germakht*	home-made
Hering	*hairing*	herring
Himbeeren	*himbairen*	raspberries
Hirschmedaillons	*heersh-medayohngs*	venison fillets
Honig	*hohnig*	honey
Huhn	*hoon*	chicken
Hühnerbrühe	*hewnerbrewer*	chicken broth
Hummer	*hoomer*	lobster
Kaffee	*kafai*	coffee
Kartoffelpuffer	*kaartoffel-puffer*	potato fritters
Käse	*kaiser*	cheese
Käsekuchen	*kaizer-kookhen*	cheesecake
Kassler	*kassler*	braised smoked pork chop
Kirschen	*keershen*	cherries
Kokosnuss	*kohkosnoos*	coconut
Königsberger Klopse	*kurnigsbairger klopser*	meat balls with caper sauce
Kraftbrühe	*krafft-brewer*	beef soup
Kuchen	*kookhen*	cake/gateau
Ingwer	*ingver*	ginger

Jäger	*Yaiger*	with a spicy sauce
Johannisbeeren	*Yohannis-bairen*	currants
rote	*rohter*	red
schwarze	*schvaartser*	black
Kabeljau	*kaabelYow*	cod
Kalb (-fleisch)	*kalp (-flysh)*	veal
Kalte Platte	*kalter platter*	selection of cold meats
Kaninchen	*kaneenshen*	rabbit
Karotten	*karotten*	carrots
Kartoffeln	*kaartoffeln*	potatoes
Kartoffelbrei	*kaartofferlbr-I*	mashed potatoes
Klösschen	*klursshen*	dumplings
Knackwurst	*knakvoorst*	type of Frankfurter
Knoblauch	*knohb-lowkh*	garlic
Kohl	*kohl*	cabbage
Kopfsalat	*kopfzalaat*	lettuce
Kotelett	*kohtelet*	chop/cutlet
Krabben	*krabben*	shrimps/prawns
Kräuter	*kroyter*	herbs
Krebs	*krebz*	crab
Lachs	*lakhs*	salmon
Lamm (-fleisch)	*lam (-flysh)*	lamb
Lauch	*lowkh*	leek
Leber	*laiber*	liver
Leipziger Allerlei	*lyptsiger alerly*	mixed vegetables

Limone	*limohner*	lime
Linsen	*linzen*	lentils
Mais	*mys*	sweetcorn
Makrele	*makrailer*	mackerel
Mandarine	*mandareener*	mandarin/tangerine
Mandeln	*mandeln*	almonds
Medaillons	*medayohngs*	small fillets of meat
Meeresfrüchte	*maires-frewshter*	seafood
Meerrettichsoße	*mairrettish-sohsser*	horseradish sauce
Melone	*melohner*	melon
zum Mitnehmen	*tsoom mitnaimen*	to take away
Möhren	*muren*	carrots
Mohrrüben	*mohrewben*	carrots
Mokka	*moka*	coffee
Mus	*moos*	puree
MwSt (Mehrwertsteuer)	*mair-vairt-stoyer*	VAT
Nachspeisen	*nakh-shpyzen*	desserts
Nieren	*neeren*	kidneys
Nudeln	*noodeln*	noodles
Nüsse	*newsser*	nuts
Obst	*ohbst*	fruit
Oliven	*oleeven*	olives
Olivenöl	*oleeven-url*	olive oil
Orange	*oronjer*	orange
Palatschinken	*palaat-shinken*	stuffed pancakes

Pampelmuse	*pampelmoozer*	grapefruit
paniert	*paneert*	cooked in bread crumbs
Paprikaschoten	*papreeka-shohten*	green peppers
Pellkartoffeln	*pell-kaartoffeln*	potatoes boiled in their jackets
Pfannkuchen	*pfankookhen*	pancake
Pfeffer	*pfeffer*	pepper
Pfirsich	*pfeerzish*	peach
Pflaumen	*pflowmen*	plums
Pilze	*piltser*	mushrooms
Platte	*platter*	platter, selection
Pommes frites	*pom frit*	chips (french fries)
Porree	*porai*	leek
Poularde	*poolaard*	chicken
Pute	*pooter*	turkey
Pumpernickel	*poompernickel*	dark rye bread
Püree	*pewrai*	puree
Quark	*kvaark*	curd cheese
Rahm	*raam*	cream
Radieschen	*radeeshen*	radishes
Räucherlachs	*roykher-lakhs*	smoked salmon
Reh	*rai*	venison
Reis	*rys*	rice
Rhabarber	*rabaarber*	rhubarb
Rind (-fleisch)	*rint (-flysh)*	beef

Rippchen	*ripshen*	spare ribs
Rohschinken	*roh-shinken*	cured ham
Rosenkohl	*rohzenkohl*	brussels sprouts
Rosinen	*rohzeenen*	raisins
Rostbraten	*rostbraaten*	roast
rote Beete	*rohte baite*	beetroot
Rotkohl	*rohtkohl*	red cabbage
Russische Eier	*roosisher I-er*	eggs/mayonnaise
mit/ohne Sahne	*mit/ohner zaaner*	with/without cream
Salat	*zalaat*	salad
Salatsoße	*salaat-sohser*	salad dressing
Salz	*zalts*	salt
Salzkartoffeln	*zalts-kaartoffeln*	boiled potatoes
Sardinen	*zaardeenen*	sardines
Sauerbraten	*zower-braaten*	roast marinated beef
scharf	*shaarf*	hot/highly seasoned
Schaschlik	*shashlik*	kebab
Schinken	*shinken*	ham
Schlachtplatte	*shlakhtplatter*	selection of cold meats and sausages
Schlagsahne	*shlaagzaaner*	whipped cream
Schnitzel	*shnitzel*	escalope
Schokolade	*shokohlaader*	chocolate
Scholle	*sholler*	plaice
Schwein (-efleisch)	*shvyner (-flysh)*	pork
Seezunge	*zai-tsoonger*	sole

Semmelknödel	*zemmelknurdel*	bread dumplings
Senf	*zenf*	mustard
Soße	*sohsser*	sauce
Spargel	*shpaargel*	asparagus
Speck	*shpek*	bacon
Speisekarte	*shpyzer-kaarter*	menu
Spinat	*shpinaat*	spinach
Stangensellerie	*shtangern-zeleree*	celery
Strammer Max	*shtrammer max*	ham and fried egg on bread
Suppe	*zooper*	soup
süß-sauer	*zews-zower*	sweet and sour
Süßspeisen	*zewss-shpyzern*	desserts
Tagesgericht	*taages-gerisht*	dish of the day
Tagesmenü	*taages-menew*	menu of the day
Teig	*tyg*	pastry
Teigwaren	*tyg-vaaren*	pasta
Thunfisch	*toonfish*	tuna
Tomaten	*tomaaten*	tomatoes
Torte	*torter*	gâteau/flan
Truthahn	*troothaan*	turkey
überbacken	*ewberbacken*	au gratin, lightly grilled
vegetarisch	*vegetaarish*	vegetarian
vom Grill	*fomm grill*	grilled
Vorspeisen	*fohr-shpyzen*	starters, hors d'oeuvre
Walnuss	*vaalnooss*	walnut

Wassermelone	*vassermelohner*	watermelon
Weintrauben	*vyntrowben*	grapes
Weißkohl	*vyskohl*	white cabbage
Wiener Schnitzel	*veener shnitzel*	veal escalope
Wild	*vilt*	game/venison
würzig	*vewrtsig*	spicy
Wurstplatte	*voorstplatter*	selection of cold sausage
Würze	*vewrtser*	seasoning/spice
Zander	*tsander*	pike-perch, zander
Zitrone	*tsitrohner*	lemon
Zucchini	*tsookhini*	courgettes
Zucker	*tsooker*	sugar
Zwiebeln	*tsveebeln*	onions
Zwetschgen	*tsvechgen*	plums
Zwiebelkuchen	*tsveebel-kookhen*	onion tart

ENTERTAINMENT AND SPORT

• You can find out what's on from the tourist office, or from the local newspaper.

• Films are usually dubbed into German rather than subtitled.

• The German-speaking countries are well-known for their winter sports facilities. Germany has resorts not only in the Alps, but also in the Black Forest (*Schwarzwald*), and the Harz Mountains. Both downhill (*Abfahrtslauf*) and cross-country skiing (*Langlauf*) are popular.

 Many more towns than in Britain have a theatre and concert hall, and opera or ballet companies. Booking is usually advisable.

WHAT'S ON?

What is there to do this evening?	Was kann man heute Abend unternehmen? *vas kan man hoyter aabent oonter-naimen?*
I'm interested in...	Ich interessiere mich für... *ish interesseerer mish fewr...*
...classical music	...klassische Musik *klassisher moozeek*
...pop music	...Popmusik *popmoozeek*
...jazz	...Jazz *jaz*
...folk music	...Volksmusik *Folks-moozeek*
...films	...Filme *filmer*
I'd like to go...	Ich möchte...gehen *ish murshter...gai-en*
...to the cinema	...ins Kino... *ins keeno...*
...to a club	...in eine Disko... *in I-ner Diskoh...*
...to a nightclub	...in einen Nachtclub... *in I-nen nakht-kloob...*
...to the theatre	...ins Theater... *ins tai-aater...*
...to a concert	...in ein Konzert... *in I-n kontsairt...*
...to the opera	...in die Oper... *in dee ohper...*
...the ballet	...ins Ballett... *ins balett...*

Can you recommend a club/ a nightclub?	Können Sie eine Disko/ einen Nachtclub empfehlen? *kurnen zee I-ner diskoh/I-nen nakht-kloob empfailen?*
Are there any tickets for this evening/ tomorrow?	Gibt es Karten für heute Abend/morgen? *gipt es kaarten fewr hoyter aabent/ morgen?*
How much are the tickets?	Was kosten die Karten? *vas kosten dee kaarten?*
When does it begin?	Wann beginnt es? *van bergint es?*
When does it end?	Wann ist es zu Ende? *van ist es tsoo ender?*
I'd like 1/ 2 tickets...	Ich möchte eine Karte/ 2 Karten... *ish murshter I-ner kaarter/ tsvy kaarten...*
...for this evening	...für heute Abend *fewr hoyter aabent*
...for tomorrow	...für morgen *fewr mohrgen*
...in the circle/ stalls	...im Rang/Parkett *im rang/parket*

You may hear:

Ich empfehle... *Ish empfailer...*	I recommend...
Die Plätze sind ausverkauft *dee pletser zint owsfairkowft*	The tickets are sold out
Es gibt nur noch ein paar Plätze *Es gipt noor nokh I-n paar pletser*	There are just a few tickets left

CONCERTS, OPERA, BALLET

What's being played?	Was wird gespielt?
	vas veert gershpeelt?
Which opera/ ballet is being performed?	Welche Oper/ welches Ballett wird aufgeführt?
	velsher ohper/ velshes balett veert owf-gerfewrt?
Who's the soloist/ conductor?	Wer ist der Solist/ Dirigent?
	vair ist dair zolist/ dirigent?
When is the interval?	Wann ist die Pause?
	van ist dee powzer?
How long does the interval last?	Wie lange dauert die Pause?
	vee langer dowert dee powzer?

CINEMAS AND THEATRES

What's on at the cinema?	Was läuft im Kino?
	vas loyft im keenoh?
What's on at the theatre?	Was wird im Theater aufgeführt?
	vas veert im tai-aarter owfgerfewrt?
What sort of film/ play is it?	Was für ein Film/ Stück ist es?
	vas fewr I-n film/ shtewk ist es?
Is it...?	Ist es...?
	ist es...?
...a comedy	...eine Komödie
	I-ner kommurdi-er
...a musical	...ein Musical
	I-n 'musical'
...a horror film	...ein Horrorfilm
	I-n horohrfilm
...a thriller	...ein Krimi
	I-n krimmi

...a German film	...ein deutscher Film *I-n do̲ycher film*
...subtitled	...mit Untertiteln *mit o̲onter-teetln*
...dubbed	...synchronisiert *zewn-khronize̲ert*
Who is in it?	Wer sind die Schauspieler? *vair zint dee sho̲w-shpeeler?*
Who wrote the play?	Wer hat das Stück geschrieben? *vair hat das shtewk gershre̲eben?*
Where is the cloakroom?	Wo ist die Garderobe? *voh ist dee gaarder-ro̲hber?*
May I have a programme?	Kann ich bitte ein Programm haben? *kan ish bi̲tter I-n prohgra̲m ha̲aben?*

You may see:

Veranstaltungen	Events
Vorverkauf (-sstelle)	Advance booking (-office)
heute	Today
ausverkauft	Sold out
Letzte Vorstellung	Last showing (of film)
Nächste Aufführung	Next performance (of play, etc.)

RELAXING WITH FRIENDS

Would you like to come over...?	Möchtest du...zu uns kommen? *mu̲rshtest doo...tsoo oons ko̲mmen?*
...this evening...	...heute Abend... *ho̲yter a̲abent...*

...tomorrow...	...morgen... *mohrgen...*
...on Saturday...	...am Samstag... *am zamztaag...*
...for a glass of wine/beer...	...auf ein Glas Wein/Bier... *owf I-n glaas vyn/beer...*
...for lunch...	...zum Mittagessen... *tsoom mitaag-essen...*
...for dinner...	...zum Abendessen... *tsoom aabentessen...*
...to a party...	...auf eine Party... *owf I-ner partee...*
At what time?	Um wie viel Uhr? *oom veefeel oor?*
At eight	Um acht *oom akht*
At about nine	Gegen neun *gaigen noyn*
I'm afraid we must leave now	Leider müssen wir jetzt gehen *lyder mewsen veer Yetst gai-en*
It was lovely	Es war schön *es vaar shurn*
I've enjoyed it!	Es hat mir Spaß gemacht! *es hat meer shpass germakht!*

SPORT

I'd like to see...	Ich möchte...sehen *ish murshter...sai-en*
...a football match...	...ein Fußballspiel... *I-n foosbal-shpeel...*
...a tennis match...	...ein Tennisspiel... *I-n tennis-shpeel...*

...some horse-racing	...ein Pferderennen... *I-n pfairder-rennen...*
Is there ... near here?	Gibt es ... in der Nähe? *gipt es... in dair nai-er?*
...a golf course...	...einen Golfplatz... *I-nen golf-plats...*
...a tennis course...	...einen Tennisplatz... *I-nen tennis-plats...*
...a swimming pool...	...ein Schwimmbad... *I-n shvimmbaat...*
Do you have to be a member?	Muss man Mitglied sein? *Mooss man mitgleet zyn?*
Who's playing?	Wer spielt? *vair shpeelt?*
When does it start?	Wann beginnt es? *van berginnt es?*
How much are the tickets?	Was kostet der Eintritt? *vas kostet dair I-ntrit?*
Can you get me a ticket?	Können Sie mir eine Karte besorgen? *kurnen zee meer I-ner kaarter berzohrgen?*
Can you get us some tickets?	Können Sie uns Karten besorgen? *kurnen zee oons kaarten berzohrgen?*
What are the opening times?	Wie sind die Öffnungszeiten? *vee zint dee urfnoongstsyten?*
Is it an open-air or an indoor pool?	Ist es ein Freibad oder ein Hallenbad? *ist es I-n frybaat ohder I-n hallenbaat?*
Is it heated?	Ist es geheizt? *ist es gerhytst?*

Can one swim in the lake/ river?	Kann man im See/Fluss schwimmen? *kan man im zai/ floos shvimmen?*
Is there any fishing near here?	Kann man hier in der Nähe angeln? *kan man heer in dair nai-er angeln?*
Do I need a fishing permit?	Braucht man einen Angelschein? *browkht man I-nen angelshyn?*
How do I get a permit?	Wie bekomme ich einen Schein? *vee berkommer ish I-nen shyn?*
I'd like to play...	Ich möchte...spielen *ish murshter...shpeelen*
Where can we play...?	Wo können wir...spielen? *vo kurnen veer...shpeelen?*
Can I play...?	Kann ich...spielen? *kan ish...shpeelen?*
...golf...	...Golf... *golf...*
...tennis...	...Tennis... *tennis...*
...football...	...Fußball... *foosbal...*
What does it cost per...?	Was kostet es pro...? *vas kostet es pro...?*
...day	...Tag *taag*
...game/ round	...Spiel *shpeel*
...hour	...Stunde *shtoonder*

Can I hire...?	Kann ich....mieten?
	kan ish...meeten?
I'd like to hire...	Ich möchte...mieten
	ish murshter...meeten
Where can I hire...?	Wo kann ich...mieten?
	vo kan ish...meeten?
...a bicycle...	...ein Fahrrad...
	I-n faarraat...
...a boat...	...ein Boot...
	I-n boot...
...equipment...	...eine Ausrüstung...
	I-ner owsrewstoong...
...a windsurf board...	...ein Windsurfbrett...
	I-n vintsoorf-brett...

THE BEACH

Can you recommend a beach?	Können Sie einen Strand empfehlen?
	kurnen zee I-nen shtrant empfailen?
Is it safe for children?	Ist es für Kinder ungefährlich?
	ist es fewr kinnder oon-gerfairlish?
Is it safe for swimming?	Kann man hier ohne Gefahr schwimmen?
	kan man heer ohner gerfaar schvimmen?
Is there a lifeguard?	Gibt es eine Strandwache?
	gipt es I-ner shtrant-vakher?
When is the high tide/ low tide?	Wann ist Flut/ Ebbe?
	van ist floot/ebber?
I want to hire...	Ich möchte...mieten
	ish murshter...meeten

The coasts of Germany, facing the North Sea and the Baltic, have many miles of sandy beaches and dunes. These can be rather windy, so it is worth hiring a *Strandkorb*, a wicker chair with a hood.

...a deck-chair...

...einen Liegestuhl...
I-nen leeger-shtool...

...a sailing boat...

...ein Segelboot...
I-nen saigel-boot...

...a sunshade...

...einen Sonnenschirm...
I-nen zonnen-sheerm...

...a surfboard...

...ein Surfbrett...
I-n zoorf-bret...

You may hear:

Es ist (nicht) gefährlich
es ist (nisht) gerfairlish

It's (not) dangerous

You may see:

Angeln verboten	No fishing
Baden verboten	No swimming
Bootsverleih	Boat hire
Eisstadion	Ice rink
Fahrradweg	Cycle path
FKK-Strand	Nudist beach
Freibad	Open-air swimming pool
Gefahr	Danger
Hallenbad	Indoor swimming pool
Lawinengefahr	Danger of avalanches
Privatstrand	Private beach
Tennisplätze	Tennis courts
Zuschauer	Spectators
Zum Skilift	To the skilift

WINTER SPORTS

I want to hire...	Ich möchte...mieten *ish murshter...meeten*
...a complete set of ski equipment...	...eine komplette Skiausrüstung... *I-ner kompletter shee-owsrewstoong...*
...skis...	...Skier... *shee-er...*
...ski boots...	...Skistiefel... *shee-shteeferl...*
Can I take skiing lessons?	Kann ich Skiunterricht nehmen? *kan ish shee-oonterisht naimen?*
Are there...?	Gibt es...? *gipt es...?*
...ski-runs for beginners	...Skipisten für Anfänger *shee-peesten fewr anfenger*
...ski-runs for advanced skiers	...Skipisten für Fortgeschrittene *sheepeesten fewr fortgershrittener*
...ski-lifts	...Skilifte *sheelifter*
How much does a daily/ weekly lift pass cost?	Was kostet eine Tageskarte/ Wochenkarte für den Lift? *vas kostet I-ner taages-karter/vokhen-kaarter fewr dain lift?*
What are the snow conditions like?	Wie sind die Schneeverhältnisse? *vee zint dee shnai-fairheltnisser?*

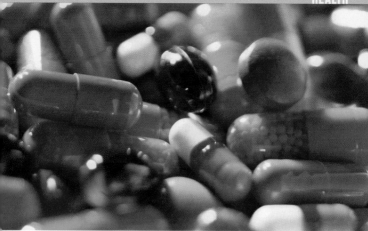

HEALTH

When travelling to Switzerland, you need to take out health insurance.

Chemists (*Apotheke*) will give advice and every town has its duty chemist open all night and at the weekend.

For emergency telephone numbers, see page 154.

AT THE DOCTOR'S

My...hurts	...tut mir weh
	toot meer vai
...arm...	Der Arm...
	dair aarm...

As Germany and Austria are in the European Union, UK visitors are entitled to free medical and dental treatment, even if they have no private holiday insurance (which is, in any case, a useful back-up). Full details are given in the booklet which accompanies the E111 form which you can get from any Post Office.

...back...	Der Rücken... *dair re__w__ken...*
...chest...	Die Brust... *dee broost...*
...eye...	Das Auge... *das __ow__ger...*
...head...	Der Kopf... *dair kopf...*
...leg...	Das Bein... *das byn...*
...stomach...	Der Magen... *dair m__aa__gen...*
...neck...	Der Hals... *dair hals...*
...foot...	Der Fuss... *dair foos...*
I've been bitten (animal)	Ich bin gebissen worden *ish bin gerb__i__ssen w__o__rden*
I've been stung	Ich bin gestochen worden *ish bin gerst__o__khen w__o__rden*
He/ she is...	Er/sie... *air/zee*
...unconscious	...ist bewusstlos *ist berv__oo__stlohss*
...bleeding	...blutet *bl__oo__tet*
...seriously injured	...ist schwer verletzt *ist shvair fairl__e__tst*
I've got...	Ich habe... *ish h__aa__ber...*
...asthma	...Asthma *__a__stma*

...a chest pain	...Brustschmerzen *br**oo**stshmairtsen*
...a cold	...eine Erkältung *I-ner airk**e**ltoong*
...a cough	...Husten *h**oo**sten*
...earache	...Ohrenschmerzen *oh**r**en-shmairtsen*
...something in my eye	...etwas in meinem Auge *etvas in m**y**nem **ow**ger*
...hayfever	...Heuschnupfen *h**oy**shnoopfen*
...a migraine	...Migräne *migr**ai**ner*
...period pains	...Menstruationsbeschwerden *menstroo-atsi**oh**ns-bershvairden*
...a rash	...einen Ausschlag *I-nen **ow**s-shlaag*
...a sore throat	...Halsschmerzen *h**a**ls-shmairtsen*
...sunstroke	...einen Sonnenstich *I-nen z**o**nnen-shtish*
Can you fetch a doctor?	Können Sie einen Arzt holen? *k**u**rnen zee I-nen **aa**rtst h**o**hlen?*
I feel faint/ sick	Ich fühle mich schwach/ schlecht *ish f**ew**ler mish shvakh/ schlesht*
I feel dizzy	Mir ist schwindelig *meer ist shv**i**nderlig*
I've got diarrhoea/ a temperature	Ich habe Durchfall/ Fieber *ish haaber d**oo**rshfall/ f**ee**ber*
I've been sick	Ich habe mich übergeben *ish h**aa**ber mish ewberg**ai**ben*

It hurts...	Es tut weh... *es toot vai...*
...all the time	...die ganze Zeit *dee gantser tsyt*
...when I do this	...wenn ich das mache *ven ish das makher*
I am...	Ich bin... *ish bin...*
...diabetic	...Diabetiker *diabaitiker*
...epileptic	...Epileptiker *Epileptikker*
...pregnant	...schwanger *shvanger*
...allergic to antibiotics/ penicillin	...allergisch gegen Antibiotika/ Penizillin *alairgish gaigen antibiohtika/ penitsileen*
I'm on the Pill	Ich nehme die Pille *ish naimer dee piller*
I had a heart attack	Ich hatte einen Herzinfarkt *ish hatter I-nen hairtsinfaarkt*
I need a prescription for...	Ich brauche ein Rezept für... *ish browkher I-n retsept fewr...*
Is it serious?	Ist es schlimm? *ist es shlim?*
Could you tell my family/ hotel?	Können Sie bitte meine Familie/ mein Hotel benachrichtigen? *kurnen zee bitter myner fameelier/ myn hotel bernakhrishtigen?*
I've been in pain...	Ich habe Schmerzen seit... *ish haaber shmairtsen zyt...*

...for several days	...einigen Tagen *I-nigen taagen*
...since yesterday	...gestern *gestern*
...since this morning	...heute morgen *hoyter mohrgen*
...for a few hours	...einigen Stunden *I-nigen shtoonden*
May I have a receipt for my insurance company?	Kann ich eine Quittung für meine Krankenkasse haben? *kan ish I-ner kvittoong fewr myner kranken-kasser haaben?*
May I have a medical certificate?	Kann ich einen Krankenschein haben? *kan ish I-nen kranken-shyn haaben?*
Could you sign this please?	Können Sie das bitte unterschreiben? *kurnen zee das bitter oonter-shryben?*

You may see:

Alle Kassen	All health insurance patients
Arzt/Ärztin für... Allgemeinmedizin	General Practitioner
Facharzt/Fachärztin für...	Specialist in...
Krankenhaus/Klinik	Hospital
Krankenwagen	Ambulance
Medikament(e)	medicine(s)
Nach Vereinbarung	By appointment
Notarzt	Emergency Doctor
Sprechstunde	surgery

| Untersuchung | check-up |
| Wartezimmer | waiting room |

You may hear:

Ich gebe Ihnen…
ish gaiber eenen

I'll give you…

…eine Spritze
I-ner shpritser

…an injection

…einen Salbe
I-ner zalber

…some ointment

…ein Rezept
I-n retsept

…a prescription

…ein Schmerzmittel
I-n shmairtsmittel

…a painkiller

Wo tut es weh?
voh toot es vai?

Where does it hurt?

Wie lange geht es Ihnen
schon so?
*vee langer gait es eenen
shohn so?*

How long have you been
feeling like this?

Tief atmen, bitte
teef aatmen, bitter

Breathe deeply, please

Husten Sie, bitte
hoosten zee bitter

Cough, please

Sie müssen…Tage lang im
Bett bleiben
*zee mewssen…taager lang im
bet blyben*

You must stay in bed for…days

Sie müssen ins Krankenhaus
gehen
*zee mewssen ins krankenhows
gai-en*

You must go to hospital

Es ist…	It's…
es ist…	
…eine Blinddarmentzündung	…appendicitis
I-ner blint-darment-tsewndoong	
…eine Gehirnerschütterung	…concussion
I-ner gerheern-ershewtteroong	
…eine Grippe	…flu
I-ner gripper	
…eine Lebensmittelvergiftung	…food poisoning
I-ner laibenzmittel-fairgiftoong	
…eine Magenverstimmung	…an stomach upset
I-ner maagen-fairshtimmoong	
…ein Sonnenstich	…sunstroke
I-n zonnen-shtish	
…gebrochen	…broken/ fractured
gerbrokhen	
…infiziert	…infected
infitseert	
…verrenkt	…dislocated
fairrenkt	
…verstaucht	…sprained
fairshtowkht	
Sie sollten zum Arzt gehen	You'll need to see a doctor
zee zollten tsoom aartst gehen	
Sie brauchen ein Rezept dafür	You need a prescription for
zee browkhen I-n Retsept dafewr	that
Nehmen Sie jeweils … Tabletten	Take … tablets at a time
naimen zee yaivyls … tabletten	
Einmal/zweimal täglich	Once/twice a day
I-nmaal/tsvymaal taiglish	
vor/nach dem Essen	before/after meals
fohr/nakh daim essen	

Was nehmen Sie sonst?
vas naimen zee zonst?

What else do you take?

Sie müssen zum Röntgen gehen
zee mewssen tsoom rurntgen gai-en

You'll need to have it x-rayed

Sie müssen operiert werden
zee mewssen operiert vairden

You'll need to have an operation

AT THE DENTIST

I've got toothache

Ich habe Zahnschmerzen
ish haaber tsaan-shmairtsen

Can you recommend a dentist?

Können Sie einen Zahnarzt empfehlen?
kurnen zee I-nen tsaan-artst empfailen?

Can I make an appointment?

Kann ich einen Termin haben?
kan ish I-nen tairmeen haaben?

It's urgent

Es ist dringend
es ist dringent

I've lost a filling/ crown

Ich habe eine Plombe/ eine Krone verloren
ish haaber I-ner plomber/ I-ner krohner fairlohren

It's this tooth

Es ist dieser Zahn
es ist deezer tsaan

Can you give me an anaesthetic?

Können Sie mir eine Spritze geben?
kurnen zee meer I-ner spritzer gaiben?

I've broken my denture

Ich habe meine Prothese zerbrochen
Ish haaber myner prohtaizer zerbrokhen

Can you repair it?

Können Sie es reparieren?
kurnen zee es parpareeren?

How long will it take?	Wie lange dauert es? *vee langer dowert es?*
I'm insured	Ich bin versichert *ish bin fairsishert*

You may hear:

Welcher Zahn tut Ihnen weh?
velsher tsaan toot eenen vai?

Which tooth hurts?

SHOPPING AND SERVICES

• Opening times are as follows:

	Weekdays	Saturdays
Germany	8/9am to 6/6.30pm	8/9am to 12/2pm
Austria	8/9am to 6/6.30pm	8/9am to 12/2pm
Switzerland	8/9am to 6/6.30pm	8/9am to 4/5pm

• Some shops close for lunch.

• Bookshops and stationers are usually separate. Magazines and newspapers can be bought at news-stands and at many bookshops.

• Chemists (*Apotheke*) sell only medicines and health items. For toiletries, films etc, look for a *Drogerie*.

 In Germany, shops stay open untill 6pm on the first Saturday of every month.
In Switzerland, shops are often closed on Monday morning.

SHOPPING

Where can I buy...?	Wo kann ich ... kaufen? *voh kan ish ... kowfen?*
I'm looking for...	Ich suche... *ish zookher*
I'm just looking	Ich sehe mich nur um *ish sai-er mish noor oom*
Can you help me?	Können Sie mir helfen? *kurnen zee meer helfen?*
Do you have any ...?	Haben Sie ...? *haaben zee ...?*
Where is the...?	Wo ist...? *voh ist...?*
...lift	...der Fahrstuhl *dair faar-shtool*
...escalator	...die Rolltreppe *dee rol-trepper*
...till/check-out	...die Kasse *dee kasser*
Where are the ...?	Wo finde ich...? *voh finder ish...?*
I saw it in the window	Ich habe es im Fenster gesehen *ish haaber es im fenster gersai-en*
That one/those	Das da/die da *das daa/dee daa*
Do you have any others?	Haben Sie noch andere? *haaben zee nokh anderer?*
Do you have any more?	Haben Sie noch mehr davon? *haaben zee nokh mair daafon?*
Do you have it in any other colours?	Haben Sie es in anderen Farben? *haaben zee es in anderen faarben?*

It's for a present	Es ist ein Geschenk *es is I-n gershenk*
I'm looking for something (a bit)...	Ich suche etwas (ein bisschen)... *ish zookher etvas (I-n biss-shen)*
...cheaper	...Billigeres *billigeres*
...better	...Besseres *besseres*
...darker	...Dunkleres *doonkleres*
...lighter (colour)	...Helleres *helleres*
...larger	...Größeres *grursseres*
...smaller	...Kleineres *klyneres*
I may come back later	Ich komme vielleicht später zurück *ish kommer feelysht shpaiter tsoorewk*
I (don't) like it	Es gefällt mir (nicht) *es gerfelt meer (nisht)*
May I try it/them on?	Darf ich es/sie anprobieren? *darf ish es/zee anprobeeren?*
I'll take it/them	Ich nehme es/sie *ish naimer es/zee*
I prefer that one	ich mag diesen lieber *ish maag deezen leeber*
Will you gift wrap it, please?	Können Sie es als Geschenk einpacken, bitte? *kurnen zee es als gershenk I-npaken, bitter?*
It's not what I'm looking for	Es ist nicht das, was ich suche *es ist nisht das, vas ish zookher*

PAYING

Where is the till/check out?	Wo ist die Kasse? *voh ist dee kasser?*
How much is it?	Wie viel kostet es? *veefeel kostet es?*
Do you take credit cards/ traveller's cheques?	Nehmen Sie Kreditkarten/ Reiseschecks? *naimen zee kredeet-karten/ ryzer-sheks?*
Is VAT included?	Ist Mehrwertsteuer inbegriffen? *ist mairvairt-shtoyer inbergriffen?*
Can you order it for me?	Können Sie es mir bitte bestellen? *kurnen zee es meer bitter berstellen?*
Can you send it to this address?	Können Sie es an diese Adresse schicken? *kurnen zee es an deezer adresser schicken?*
Can you deliver it?	Können Sie es liefern? *kurnen zee es leefern?*
How long will it take?	Wie lange dauert es? *vee langer dowert es?*
Could you wrap it as a present?	Können Sie es als Geschenk einpacken? *kurnen zee ess als gershenk I-npacken?*

You may hear:

Kann ich Ihnen helfen? *kan ish eenen helfen?*	Can I help you?
Werden Sie schon bedient? *vairden zee shohn berdeent?*	Are you being served?

Sonst noch etwas? *zonst nokh etvas?*	Anything else?
Wie viel/wie viele möchten Sie? *veefeel/veefeeler murshten zee?*	How much/how many would you like?
Möchten Sie es/sie anprobieren? *murshten zee es/zee anprobeeren?*	Would you like to try it on?
Welche Farbe/Größe möchten Sie? *velsher faarber/grursser murshten zee?*	What colour/size would you like?

PROBLEMS

I think you've made a mistake (on the bill)	Ich glaube, Sie haben sich verrechnet *ish glowber, zee haaben zish fair-reshnet*
I'd like to exchange this	Ich möchte das umtauschen *ish murshter das oomtowshen*
It's…	Es ist… *es ist…*
…the wrong size	…die falsche Größe *dee falsher grursser*
…faulty	…defekt *defekt*
I'd like a refund	Ich möchte mein Geld zurück-bekommen *ish murshter myn gelt tsoorewk-berkommen*
Here's the receipt	Hier ist die Quittung *heer ist dee kvitoong*
I bought it yesterday	Ich habe es gestern gekauft *ish haaber es gestern gerkowft*
It was a present	Es war ein Geschenk *es war I-n gershenk*

Where can I get this repaired?	Wo kann ich das reparieren lassen? *voh kann ish das repar__ee__ren l__a__ssen?*
When will it/will they be ready?	Wann ist es/sind sie fertig? *van ist es/zint zee f__ai__rtig?*

You may see:

Abteilung	department
Ausgang	exit
Ausverkauf	sale
ausverkauft	sold out
Campingzubehör	camping
Eingang	entrance
Heimwerkerbedarf	DIY
Lebensmittel	groceries
Mode	fashion
nicht berühren	do not touch
Obergeschoss	upper floor
Preis	price
preiswert	good value
reduziert	reduced
Schreibwaren	stationery
Selbstbedienung	self-service
Sommerschlussverkauf	summer sale
Sonderangebot	special offer
Sonderpreis	special price
Spielwaren	toys
Süßwaren	sweets
Umtausch nur gegen Quittung	goods exchanged only with receipt

vergriffen	out of stock
Winterschlussverkauf	winter sale
Zeitungen/Zeitschriften	newspapers/magazines

SHOPS

| Where's the...? | | Wo ist...? |
| | | *voh ist...?* |

...baker's	...die Bäckerei	*dee beker-I*
...bank	...die Bank	*dee bank*
...bookshop	...die Buchhandlung	*dee bookh-handloong*
...butcher's	...die Metzgerei	*dee metsger-I*
...cake-shop	...die Konditorei	*dee konditohr-I*
...camera shop	...das Fotogeschäft	*das fohto-gersheft*
...chemist's	...die Apotheke	*dee apotaiker*
...chemist's (non-dispensing)	...die Drogerie	*dee drohgeree*
...department store	...das Kaufhaus	*das kowf-hows*
...dry cleaner's	...die chemische Reinigung	*dee kaimisher runigoong*
...greengrocer's	...die Gemüsehandlung	*dee germewser-handloong*
...grocer's	...das Lebensmittelgeschäft	*das laibensmittel-gersheft*
...hypermarket	...der Großmarkt	*dair grohss-markt*
...jeweller's	...der Juwelier	*dair Yooveleer*
...laundrette	...der Waschsalon	*dair vash-zalon*
...newsagent's	...der Zeitungshändler	*dair tsytoongs-hendler*
...optician	...der Optiker	*dair optiker*
...post office	...das Postamt	*das posstamt*
...supermarket	...der Supermarkt	*dair zoopermarket*
...toy shop	...das Spielwarengeschäft	*das shpeelvaaren-gersheft*
...travel agent	...das Reisebüro	*das ryzer-bewroh*

AT A DEPARTMENT STORE

Where are the...?	Wo sind die...? *voh zint dee...?*
...CDs	...CDs *sai-daiz*
...sports goods	...Sportartikel *shport-artikel*
...books	...Bücher *bewsher*
Which floor?	In welchem Stock? *in velshem shtok?*
On the ground floor	Im Erdgeschoss *im airdgershoss*
In the basement	Im Untergeschoss *im oontergershoss*
On the first/second floor	Im ersten/zweiten Stock *im airsten/tsvyten shtok*
Toiletries	Toilettenartikel *twaletten-artikel*
Clothing and Shoes	Kleider und Schuhe *klyder oont shooer*
Electrical Goods	Elektrowaren *elektrovaaren*
Food	Lebensmittel *laibenzmittel*
Photographic Equipment	Fotoartikel *fohto-artikel*
Repairs	Reparaturen *reparatooren*

CLOTHES AND SHOES

I'd like something...	Ich möchte etwas... *ish murshter etvas...*
...for me/her/him	...für mich/sie/ihn *fewr mish/zee/een*
...to match this	...was dazu passt *vas datsoo passt*
I take size...	Ich habe Größe... *ish haaber grursser...*
(Where) can I try it on?	(Wo) kann ich es anprobieren? *(voh) kan ish es anprobeeren?*
Is there a mirror?	Gibt es einen Spiegel? *gipt es I-nen shpeegel?*
It doesn't fit	Es sitzt nicht sehr gut *es zitst nisht zair goot*
It's too...	Es ist zu... *es ist tsoo...*
...long/short	...lang/kurz *lang/koorts*
...tight/loose	...eng/weit *eng/vyt*
...big/small	...groß/klein *grohs/klyn*
Can you alter it?	Können sie es ändern? *kurnen zee es endern?*
I don't like the style/colour	Der Stil/die Farbe gefällt mir nicht *dair shteel/dee faarber gerfelt meer nisht*
Do you have this in green?	Haben Sie das in grün? *haaben zee das in grewn?*

Does it have to be handwashed?	Muss man das mit der Hand waschen?
	moos man das mit dair hant vashen?

You may hear:

Welche Größe haben Sie?	What size do you take?
velsher grurser haaben zee?	
Wir haben es nicht in dieser Farbe/Ihrer Größe	We don't have it in that colour/your size
veer haaben es nisht in deezer faarber/eerer grurser	
Der Spiegel/die Umkleidekabine ist da drüben	The mirror/fitting room is over there
dair shpeegel/dee oomklyderkabeener ist da drewben	

COLOURS AND FABRICS

black	schwarz	blue	blau
	shvarts		*bl-ow*
brown	braun	green	grün
	brown		*grewn*
orange	orange	yellow	gelb
	oronzher		*gelp*
red	rot	white	weiß
	roht		*vys*
light (grey)	hell (grau)	dark (pink)	dunkel (rosa)
	hell (grow)		*doonkel (rohza)*
cotton	Baumwolle	wool	Wolle
	bowmvoller		*voller*
leather	Leder	silk	Seide
	laider		*zyder*
suede	Wildleder	synthetic	synthetisch
	viltlaider		*zewntaitish*

SHOES

I'd like a pair of...	Ich möchte ein Paar...
	ish mur̲shter I-n paar...
...shoes	...Schuhe
	sho̲o-er
...boots	...Stiefel
	shte̲efel
...trainers	...Turnschuhe
	to̲orn-shooer
...walking boots	...Wanderschuhe
	va̲nder-shooer
Do you have a larger/ smaller pair?	Haben Sie ein größeres/ kleineres Paar?
	ha̲aben zee I-n gru̲rseres/ kly̲neres paar?
Do you have any...?	Haben Sie...?
	ha̲aben zee...?
...insoles	...Einlegesohlen
	I̲-nlaiger-zohlen
...laces	...Schnürsenkel
	shne̲wr-zenkel
...polish	...Schuhcreme
	sho̲o-kraimer
Can I try them on?	Kann ich sie anprobieren?
	kan ish zee a̲nprobeeren?
They're a bit uncomfortable	Sie sind ein bisschen unbequem
	zee zint I-n bi̲ss-shen o̲on-berkvaim

AT THE HAIRDRESSER'S/BARBER'S

Can you recommend a hairdresser?	Können Sie einen Friseur empfehlen?
	ku̲rnen zee I-nen frizu̲r empfa̲ilen?

Hairdresser's in Germany are normally closed on Mondays.

I'd like an appointment for...	Ich möchte einen Termin am... *ish murshter I-nen tairmeen am...*
Just a trim, please	Nur etwas nachschneiden, bitte *noor etvas nakh-shnyden, bitter*
A cut and blow-dry	Schneiden und föhnen, bitte *shnyden oont furnen, bitter*
Not too short/long	Nicht zu kurz/lang *nisht tsoo koorts/lang*
A bit more off here	Hier etwas kürzer, bitte *heer etvas kewrtser, bitter*
Would you trim my beard/moustache?	Können Sie mir bitte den Bart/den Schnurrbart stutzen? *kurnen zee meer bitter dain bart/dain shnoorbart shtootsen?*
I'd like...	Ich möchte... *ish murshter...*
...the same style again	...nochmal den gleichen Schnitt *nokhmal dain glyshen shnit*
...highlights	...Strähnchen *shtrainshen*
...conditioner	...eine Haarspülung *I-ne haar-spewloong*

PHOTOGRAPHIC

I'd like a film/two films for this camera	Ich möchte einen Film/ zwei Filme für diesen Fotoapparat *ish murshter I-nen film/tsvy filmer fewr deezen fohto-aparaat*
black and white film	Schwarzweißfilm *shvaarts-vys-film*
colour film	Farbnegativfilm *faarbnegateef-film*
colour slide film	Farbdiafilm *faarb-deeafilm*
24/36 exposures	24/36 Aufnahmen *feer-oont-tsvantsig/zekhs-oont-drysig owfnaamen*
I'd like some passport photos taken	Ich möchte Passbilder machen lassen *ish murshter pasbilder makhen lassen*
Is processing included?	Ist der Preis mit Entwicklung? *ist dair prys mit entvikloong?*
How much is processing?	Was kostet die Entwicklung? *vas kostet dee entvikloong?*
How long will it take?	Wie lange dauert es? *vee langer dowert es?*
I'd like...copies/enlargements	Ich möchte...Abzüge/ Vergrößerungen *ish murshter...aptsewger/ fairgrurseroongen*
Can you repair my camera?	Können Sie meinen Fotoapparat reparieren? *kurnen zee mynen fohto-aparaat repareeren?*

| Do you have any batteries? | Haben Sie Batterien? |
| | *haaben zee bateree-en?* |

AT THE CHEMIST'S

Where's the nearest (all-night) chemist's?	Wo ist die nächste Apotheke (mit Nachtdienst)?
	voh ist dee neshster apotaiker (mit nakhtdeenst)?
I want something for...	Ich möchte etwas gegen...
	ish murshter etvas gaigen...
...diarrhoea	...Durchfall
	doorshfal
...a headache	...Kopfschmerzen
	kopfshmairtsen
...insect-bites	...Insektenstiche
	inzektenshtisher
...a sore throat	...Halsschmerzen
	hals-shmairtsen
...sunburn	...Sonnenbrand
	zonnenbrant
...an upset stomach	...Magenverstimmung
	maagen-fairshtimoong
Do I need a prescription for it?	Brauche ich ein Rezept dafür?
	browkher ish I-n retsept dafewr?
It's for an adult/a child	Es ist für einen Erwachsenen/ein Kind
	es ist fewr I-nen airvakhsenen/I-n kint

There are two types of chemist's in Germany:
The *Apotheke* is a pharmacist's. It can make up prescriptions and sell drugs but it does not sell toiletries, films etc. When closed, the address of the nearest chemist's which is open is displayed in the window. At night ring the doorbell for service. The *Drogerie* sells toiletries, non-prescription drugs etc. N.B. *Gift* means 'poison'.

GROCERIES

• For items of food and drink, see the section beginning page 73.

Can I help myself?	Kann ich mich selbst bedienen? *kan ish mish zelbst berdeenen?*
May I have a plastic bag?	Kann ich eine Plastiktüte haben? *kan ish I-ner plastik-tewter haaben?*
one/some of those	eins/einige von denen *I-ns/I-niger von dainen*
a piece/two pieces of...	ein Stück/zwei Stück... *I-n shtewk/tsvy shtewk...*
a slice/two slices of...	eine Scheibe/zwei Scheiben... *I-ner shyber/tsvy shyben...*
a bottle of...	eine Flasche... *I-ner flasher...*
a can/tin of...	eine Dose... *I-ner dohzer...*
a jar of...	ein Glas... *I-n glaas...*
a packet of...	eine Packung/eine Tüte... *I-ner pakkoong/I-ner tewter...*
a kilo of...	ein Kilo... *I-n keelo...*
a pound of...	ein Pfund... *I-n pfoont*
half a pound of...	ein halbes Pfund... *I-n halbes pfoont...*
200 grams of...	200 Gramm... *tsvy hoondert gram...*
a litre of...	ein Liter... *I-n leeter...*

MISCELLANEOUS

I'm looking for a present for...	Ich suche ein Geschenk für... *ish sookher I-n gershenk fewr...*
Do you have anything in gold/silver?	Haben Sie etwas in Gold/Silber? *haaben zie etvas in golt/zilber?*
Is that real silver?	Ist das Echtsilber? *ist das esht-zilber?*
I want a small present	Ich möchte ein kleines Geschenk *ish murshter I-n klyn-es gershenk*
I'd like a toy/game	Ich möchte ein Spielzeug/Spiel *ish murshter I-n shpeel-tsoyg/ shpeel*
Do you have any CDs by...?	Haben Sie CDs von...? *haaben zee sai-daiz fon...?*
I'd like a souvenir	Ich möchte ein Andenken *ish murshter I-n andenken*
It's for...	Es ist für... *es ist fewr...*
...my girlfriend/boyfriend	...meine Freundin/meinen Freund *myner froyndin/mynen froynt*
...my wife/ husband	...meine Frau/meinen Mann *myner frow/mynen man*
...my parents	...meine Eltern *myner eltern*

CHURCHES AND RELIGIOUS SERVICES

Where is...?	Wo ist...? *voh ist...?*
...the Catholic church	...die katholische Kirche *dee katohlisher keersher*
...the Protestant church	...die evangelische Kirche *dee evangailisher keersher*

| ...synagogue | ...die Synagoge |
| | *dee zewnagohger* |

| At what time is...? | Wann beginnt...? |
| | *van bergint...?* |

| ...the mass | ...die Messe |
| | *dee messer* |

| ...the service | ...der Gottesdienst |
| | *dair gottesdeenst* |

| Is there a...who speaks English? | Gibt es einen..., der Englisch spricht? |
| | *gipt es I-nen ..., dair ennglish shprisht?* |

| ...minister... | ...Pfarrer... |
| | *pfarrer...* |

| ...priest... | ...Priester... |
| | *preester...* |

| ...rabbi... | ...Rabbiner.. |
| | *rabeener...* |

REPAIRS

| Can you repair this? | Können Sie das reparieren? |
| | *kurnen zee das repareeren?* |

| There's something wrong with this | Etwas stimmt nicht damit |
| | *etvas shtimt nisht daamit* |

| It works sometimes | Es funktioniert manchmal |
| | *es foonktsioneert manshmaal* |

| It doesn't work | Es funktioniert nicht |
| | *es foonktsioneert nisht* |

| It's jammed | Es klemmt |
| | *es klemt* |

| It's broken | Es ist kaputt |
| | *es ist kapoot* |

It is usually possible to go into most churches, cathedrals etc. except when a service is in progress. In many larger towns you will find some services conducted in English. Ask at the local tourist office for details.

| I can't close/open it | Ich kann es nicht zumachen/ aufmachen
ish kan es nisht tsoomakhen/ owfmakhen |
| How much will it cost? | Wie viel kostet es?
veefeel kostet es? |
| How long will it take? | Wie lange dauert es?
vee langer dowert es? |
| I'm here for two more days/weeks | Ich bin noch 2 Tage/ Wochen hier
ish bin nokh tsvy taager/ vokhen heer |
| Is it worth it? | Lohnt es sich?
lohnt es sish? |

You may hear:

| Es lohnt sich nicht
es lohnt sish nisht | It's not worth it |
| Das lässt sich nicht reparieren
das lesst sish nisht repareeren | It can't be repaired |
| Dieses Modell wird nicht mehr hergestellt
deezes model virt nisht mair hairgershtelt | This model isn't produced any more |
| Wir müssen die Ersatzteile bestellen
veer mewssen dee airzatstyler bershtellen | We'll have to order more parts |
| Es ist in 2 Tagen fertig
es ist in tsvy taagen fairtig | It'll be ready in 2 days |
| Wir müssen es wegschicken
veer mewssen es vaig-shiken | We'll have to send it away |

Am besten lassen Sie es zu
Hause reparieren
am besten lassen zee es tsoo
howzer repareeren

It would be better to have it
repaired at home

SHOES

Where can I get my shoes
mended?

Wo kann ich diese Schuhe
reparieren lassen?
voh kan ish deezer shoo-er
repareeren lassen?

Can you repair these shoes?

Können Sie diese Schuhe
reparieren?
kurnen zee deezer shoo-er
repareeren?

Can you stitch this?

Können Sie das nähen?
kurnen zee das nai-en?

I want new soles/heels

Ich möchte neue Sohlen/Absätze
ish murshter noyer sohlen/apsetser

When will they be ready?

Wann sind sie fertig?
van zint zee fairtig?

BANKS AND POST OFFICES

• Credit cards are widely used for payment in shops, restaurants and
hotels.

• When changing money in banks, it is normal to fill in the forms at
one counter, but to collect the money from another.

• Banking hours: 8.30-12.30 and 13.30-16.00 (18.00 on
Thursdays). Outside these hours look for currency exchange shops
(*Geldwechsel* or *Wechselstube*).

• Germany/Austria: 1 Euro = 100 cent

  Switzerland: I Fr (Franken) = 100 Rp (Rappen)

BANK

Where is the nearest bank?	Wo ist die nächste Bank/ Sparkasse? *voh ist dee neshster bank/ shpaarkasser?*
I'd like to change some pounds into Euros	Ich möchte Pfund in Euro wechseln *ish murshter pfoont in oyroh vekhseln*
I'd like to cash a traveller's cheque/ Eurocheque	Ich möchte einen Reisescheck/ Euroscheck einlösen *ish murshter I-nen ryzershek/oyroshek I-nlurzen*
I'd like to buy some Euros with my credit card	Ich möchte Euros mit meiner Kreditkarte kaufen *ish murshter oyrohs mit myner kredeetkaarter kowfen*
What's the exchange rate for the pound?	Wie ist der Kurs für das Pfund? *vee ist dair koorz fewr das pfoont?*
Here is my passport	Hier ist mein Pass *heer ist myn pass*
I'd like notes/some small change	Ich möchte Scheine/etwas Kleingeld *ish murshter shyner/etvas klyngelt*
Where should I sign?	Wo muss ich unterschreiben? *voh moos ish oonter-shryben?*
I'd like to deposit this money	Ich möchte dieses Geld einzahlen *ish murshter deezes Geld I-n-tsaalen*
I'd like to transfer some money	Ich möchte Geld überweisen *ish murshter gelt ewbervysen*
I'd like to withdraw some money	Ich möchte Geld abheben *ish murshter gelt abhaiben*

I'd like to open an account	Ich möchte ein Konto eröffnen
	ish murshter I-n konto air-urfnen
Where should I sign?	Wo muss ich unterschreiben?
	voh moos ish oonter-shryben?
I want to pay this into my account	Ich möchte das auf mein Konto einzahlen
	ish murshter das owf myn konto I-n-tsaalen

You may hear:

Wie viel möchten Sie wechseln?	How much would you like
veefeel murshten zee vekhlseln?	to change?
Kann ich Ihren Pass sehen?	May I see your passport?
kan ish eeren pass zai-en?	
Ohne Pass können wir Reiseschecks nicht einlösen	We can't change traveller's cheques without a passport
ohner pass kurnen veer ryzersheks nicht I-nlurzen	
Bitte füllen Sie dieses Formular aus	Please fill in this form
bitter fewlen zee deezes formoolaar ows	
Bitte unterschreiben Sie hier	Please sign here
bitter oontershryben zee heer	
Nehmen Sie dieses Papier/ diese Nummer	Take this piece of paper/ this number
naimen zee deezes papeer/ deezer noomer	
Gehen Sie an Kasse Nummer...	Go to counter number...
gai-en zee an kasser noomer...	
Wie darf ich Ihnen das Geld geben?	How would you like the money?
vee daarf ish eenen das gelt gaiben?	
Das ist Ihre Quittung	Here's your receipt
das ist eerer kvittong	

Das macht…
das makht…

That comes to…

Gehen Sie an Schalter (4)
gai-en zee an shallter (feer)

Go to counter (4)

You may see:

Bank	Bank
Devisen	Foreign currency
Geldautomat	Cash dispenser
Geldwechsel	Currency exchange
Kasse	Cash desk
Schalterstunden } Schalterzeiten	Opening hours
Sorten	Foreign currency
Sparkasse	Savings bank
Wechselstube	Currency exchange

POST OFFICE

Opening times:-

Germany
8.00-18.00; Saturday 8.00-13.00

Austria
8.00-12.00, 14.00-17.00; Saturday 8.00-11.00

Switzerland
7.30-12.00, 13.30-18.30; Saturday 8.00-11.00

Where is the nearest
post office/letterbox?

Wo ist das nächste
Postamt/der nächste
Briefkasten?
*voh ist das nehster
posstamt/dair nehster
breefkasten?*

N.B. *Spielbank* is a casino.

An 80-cent stamp, please	Eine Briefmarke zu 80 cent, bitte *I-ner breefmarker tsoo akhtsig sent, bitter*
5 1-Euro stamps, please	Fünf Briefmarken zu 1 Euro, bitte *fewnf breefmaarken tsoo I-nem oyroh bitter*
What's the cost of...?	Was kostet...? *vas kostet...?*
...a letter to America?	...ein Brief nach Amerika *I-n breef nakh amerika*
...a postcard to England	...eine Postkarte nach England *I-ner postkaarter nakh englant*
...this parcel	...dieses Paket *deezes pakait*
Can you weigh this letter/this parcel?	Können Sie bitte diesen Brief/dieses Paket wiegen? *kurnen zee bitter deezen breef/deezes pakait veegen?*
I'd like to send it...	Ich möchte es...schicken *ish murshter es...shicken*
...by air mail...	...per Luftpost... *pair looftposst...*
...express delivery...	...per Eilpost... *pair I-lposst...*
...letter post...	...als Brief... *als breef...*
...parcel post...	...als Paket... *als pakait...*
...surface mail...	...per Normaltarif... *pair normaaltareef...*

Post offices are recognisable by the word *Post(amt)* and the symbol of the post horn. Letter boxes are yellow.

...registered delivery...

...per Einschreiben...
pair I-nshryben...

Is there any post for me?

Ist Post für mich da?
ist posst fewr mish daa?

You may see:

Ausland	Foreign (counter)
ausländische Währungen	foreign currency
Auszahlungen	withdrawals
Brief(e)	letter(s)
Briefkasten	Letter box
Briefmarkenautomat	Stamp dispenser
Bundespost	Federal Post Office
Fernsprecher	Telephone
Geldwechsel	currency exchange
Nächste Leerung	Next collection
Päckchen	small parcels
Pakete	Parcels
Post(amt)	post office
Postkarte(n)	post card(s)
Postlagernde Sendungen	Post restante
Postleitzahl	post code
Postwertzeichen	Stamps
Sondermarken	Commemorative stamps

COMMUNICATIONS

TELEPHONE

• Most telephone boxes have instructions in English and German as well as diagrams. International calls can also be made from most of them, or you can go to the counter marked *Ferngespräche* in larger post offices, where you will be allocated a telephone booth. You pay after you have finished your call.

• When making phone calls abroad, remember to omit the first 0 of the area code following the country code: e.g. when phoning Cambridge from Germany, dial 0044 (England), then 1223 (not 01223), followed by the number.

Where's...?	Wo ist...?
	voh ist...?
...the telephone	...das Telefon
	das telefohn
...the nearest telephone box	...die nächste Telefonzelle
	dee neshster telefohn-tseller
May I use the phone?	Darf ich das Telefon benutzen?
	daarf ish das telefohn bernootsen?
Hallo, this is...	Hallo, hier...
	hallo, heer...
May I speak to...?	Kann ich...sprechen, bitte?
	kan ish...sphreshen bitter?
May I have extension number...?	Ich möchte Apparat...
	ish murshter aparaat...
I'll phone again later	Ich rufe wieder an
	ish roofer veeder an

On the phone, 2 is pronounced *tsvoh*, to avoid confusion with 3 *(dry)*.

When can I get him/her?	Wann kann ich ihn/sie erreichen? *van kan ish een/zee airryshen?*
Can I leave a message?	Können Sie etwas ausrichten? *kurnen zee etvas owsrishten?*
My name is...	Ich heiße... *ish hysser...*
Please tell him/her I called	Bitte sagen Sie ihm/ihr, dass ich angerufen habe *bitter zaagen zee eem/eer, das ish angeroofen haaber*
Could you ask him/her to phone me?	Können Sie ihn/sie bitten, mich anzurufen? *kurnen zee een/zee bitten, mish antsooroofen?*
between 5 and 7 o'clock	zwischen 5 und 7 Uhr *tsvishen fewnf oont zeeben oor*
My phone number is...	Meine Telefonnummer ist... *myner telefohn-noomer ist...*

OPERATOR

What's the code for...	Was ist die Vorwahl für...? *vas ist dee fohrvaal fewr...?*
I'd like to make a call to America	Ich möchte nach Amerika anrufen *ish murshter nakh amerika anroofen*
What's the number for (international) directory enquiries?	Welche Nummer hat die (internationale) Auskunft? *velsher noomer hat dee (internatsionaaler) owskoonft?*
What's the number for the (international) operator?	Welche Nummer hat die (internationale) Vermittlung? *velsher noomer hat dee (internatsionaaler) fairmitloong?*

Could you help me to get this number?	Können Sie mir helfen, diese Nummer zu bekommen? *kurnen zee meer helfen, deezer noomer tsoo berkommen?*
I can't get through	Ich komme nicht durch *ish kommer nisht doorsh*
I want to make a reverse charge call	Ich möchte ein R-Gespräch *ish murshter I-n air-gershpraish*
I've been cut off	Ich bin unterbrochen worden *ish bin oonterbrokhen vorden*
I dialled the wrong number	Ich habe mich verwählt *ish haaber mish fairvailt*
I was given the wrong number	Man hat mich falsch verbunden *man hat mish falsh verboonden*
What did the call cost?	Was hat das Gespräch gekostet? *vas hat das gershpraish gerkostet?*

ELECTRONIC

I'd like to send a fax	Ich möchte ein Fax schicken *ish murshter I-n fax shicken*
Can I send a fax/e-mail from here?	Kann ich von hier faxen/mailen? *kan ish fon heer faxen/mailen?*
What's your e-mail address/ fax number?	Wie ist Ihre E-Mail-Adresse/ Faxnummer? *vee ist eerer 'E' mail-adresser/ faxnoomer?*
Can you text me?	Können Sie mir simsen/texten? *kurnen zee meer zimzen/texten?*
What's your mobile number?	Wie ist Ihre Handy-Nummer? *vee ist eerer handi-noomer?*

You may see:

Auskunft	Enquiries
außer Betrieb	out of order

Auslandsgespräche	Foreign calls
bitte zahlen	Please insert more money
Ferngespräch/Ferngespräche	long-distance call(s)
Feuerwehr	fire brigade
Gelbe Seiten	Yellow Pages
Geldeinwurf/Geld einwerfen	insert coins
Gespräch	call
Großbritannien	Great Britain
Hörer abnehmen	lift the receiver
Krankenhaus	hospital
Inlandsgespräche	Phone calls within the country
Münzfreier Notruf	Free emergency services calls
Münzeinwurf	Insert coins
Münzrückgabe	Returned coins
Notruf	emergency phone
Ortsgespräch(e)	local call(s)
Polizei	police
Telefonkarte	phone card
Vorwahl	dialling code
wählen	to dial
Webseite(n)	website(s)

The Alphabet

a aa	**g** gai	**m** emm	**s** ess	**y** ewpsilon
b bai	**h** haa	**n** enn	**t** tai	**z** tsett
c tsai	**i** ee	**o** oh	**u** uh	**ß** ess-tsett
d dai	**j** yot	**p** pai	**v** fow	(=ss)
e ai	**k** kaa	**q** kuh	**w** vai	
f eff	**l** ell	**r** air	**x** ix	

The accent ¨ is called the **umlaut** (*oomlowt*):

ä *aa oomlowt/ ai*   ö *oh oomlowt/ ur*   ü *uh oomlowt/ ew*

How do you spell that?

Wie schreibt man das?
vee shrypt man das?

It's spelt ...

Das schreibt man ...
das shrypt man ...

You may hear:

Wer ist am Apparat?
vair ist am apparaat?

Who's speaking?

Einen Moment, bitte
I-nen moment bitter

Just a minute; hold on, please

Bleiben Sie dran
blyben zee dran

Hold the line

Er/sie ist zur Zeit nicht da
er/zee ist tsoor tsyt nisht daa

He/she isn't in at the moment

Es ist besetzt
es ist berzetst

The line's engaged

Es antwortet niemand
es antvortet neemant

There's no answer

Können Sie später wieder
anrufen?
*kurnen zee shpaiter veeder
anroofen?*

Could you phone back later?

Kann er/sie Sie zurückrufen?
kan er/zee zee tsoorewk-roofen?

Can he/she phone you back?

Kann ich ihm/ihr etwas
ausrichten?
kan ish eem/eer etvas owsrishten?

Can I give him/her a message?

Sind Sie telefonisch
zu erreichen?
zint zee telefohnish tsoo errykhen?

Can you be reached by phone?

Sie haben sich verwählt
zee haaben zish fairvailt

You've got the wrong number

Welche Nummer haben
Sie gewählt?
*velsher noomer haaben
zee gervailt?*

What number did you dial?

ESSENTIAL INFORMATION

ACCIDENT

For emergency numbers, see page 154.

Help!
Hilfe!
h<u>i</u>lfer!

Stop!
Halt!
halt!

Please send an ambulance
Bitte schicken Sie einen
Krankenwagen
*b<u>i</u>tter sh<u>i</u>cken zee <u>I</u>-nen
kr<u>a</u>nken-w<u>aa</u>gen*

There's been an accident
Es ist ein Unfall passiert
es ist I-n <u>oo</u>nfal pas<u>ee</u>rt

on the road from...to...	auf der Straße zwischen...und... *owf dair shtraasser tsvishen...oont...*
about 4km from...	ungefähr vier Kilometer von... *oon-gefair feer kilomaiter fon...*
Where's the nearest phone?	Wo ist das nächste Telefon? *vo ist das nekhster telefohn?*
Please call the police	Rufen Sie bitte die Polizei *roofen zee bitter dee polits-I*
Call a doctor quickly	Rufen Sie schnell einen Arzt *roofen zee shnell I-nen aartst*
There are people injured	Es hat Verletzte gegeben *es hat fairletster gergaiben*
Police	Polizei *polits-I*
Ambulance	Krankenwagen *krankenvaagen*
My/your registration number	meine/Ihre Autonummer *myner/eerer owtoh-noomer*
My/your name	mein/Ihr Name *myn/eer naamer*
my/your address	meine/Ihre Adresse *myner/eerer adresser*
My/your driving licence	mein/Ihr Führerschein *myn/eer fewrer-shyn*
My/your insurance company	Meine/Ihre Versicherungsgesellschaft *myner/eerer fairsikheroongs-gerselshaft*

THEFT AND LOST PROPERTY

Where is...?	Wo ist...?
	voh ist.../
...the lost property office	...das Fundbüro
	das foontbewroh
...the police station	...das Polizeirevier
	das polits-I-reveer
I'd like to report...	Ich möchte...melden
	ish murshter...melden
...a loss...	...einen Verlust...
	I-nen fairloost...
...a theft...	...einen Diebstahl...
	I-nen deepshtaal...
I've been mugged	Ich bin überfallen worden
	ish bin ewberfallen wohrden
My...has been stolen	Mein/meine...ist gestohlen worden
	myn/myner...ist gerstohlen vorden
I've lost...	Ich habe...verloren
	ish haaber...fairlohren
...my car...	... mein Auto...
	myn owtoh...
...my handbag...	... meine Handtasche...
	myner hant-tasher...
...my luggage...	... mein Gepäck...
	myn gerpeck...
...my camera...	...meinen Fotoapparat...
	mynen fohto-aparaat...
...my cheque book...	...mein Scheckheft...
	myn shek-heft...

Look for the sign *Fundamt*, *Fundbüro* or *Fundsachen*. In smaller towns, this is often the town hall. In case of thefts, go to the police station.

...my credit card...	...meine Kreditkarte... *myner kredeetkaarter...*
...money...	...Geld... *gelt...*
...my traveller's cheques...	...meine Reiseschecks... *myner ryzersheks...*
...my umbrella...	...meinen Regenschirm... *mynen raigensheerm...*
...my wallet...	...meine Brieftasche... *myner breeftasher...*
It's made of...	Es ist aus... *es ist ows...*
...cloth	...Stoff *shtoff*
...cotton	...Baumwolle *bowmvoller*
...gold	...Gold *golt*
...leather	...Leder *laider*

• For colours and fabrics, see page 128.

It's worth about...	Es ist ungefähr...wert *es ist oon-gefair...vairt*
It has my name...	Es hat meinen Namen... *es hat mynen naamen...*
...on it	...darauf *daarowf*
...inside	...darin *daarin*
I lost it at the station	Ich habe es auf dem Bahnhof verloren *ish haaber es owf daim baanhohf fairloren*

...at about 3 o'clock	...gegen 3 Uhr
	gaigen dry oor
...today	...heute
	hoyter
...yesterday	...gestern
	gestern
I don't know when/where I lost it	Ich weiß nicht, wo/wann ich es verloren habe
	ish vys nisht, voh/van ish es fairloren haaber
My room has been broken into	In mein Zimmer ist eingebrochen worden
	in myn tsimmer ist I-ngerbrochen wohrden
My car's been broken into	Mein Auto ist aufgebrochen worden
	myn owtoh ist owfgerbrochen wohrden
I've locked myself out	Ich habe mich ausgesperrt
	ish haaber mish owsgeshpairt
My son/my daughter has disappeared	Mein Sohn/meine Tochter ist verschwunden
	myn zohn/myner tokhter ist fairshvoonden

You may hear

Wo sind Sie?	Where are you?
voh sint zee?	
Können Sie ihn/sie/es beschreiben?	Can you describe him/her/it?
kurnen zee ihn bershryben?	
Wo/Wie ist das passiert?	Where/how did it happen?
voh/vee ist das passeert?	

Bleiben Sie am Apparat *bl<u>y</u>ben ze am appar<u>aa</u>t*	Please hold the line
Bitte füllen Sie dieses Formular aus *bitter <u>few</u>len zee <u>dee</u>zes formool<u>aa</u>r ows*	Please fill in this form

You may see:

Bergwacht	Mountain rescue
Erste Hilfe	First aid
Feuer	Fire
Feuerlöscher	Fire extinguisher
Fundbüro	Lost property office
Krankenhaus/Klinik	hospital
Lebensgefahr	(mortal) danger
Nachtdienst	late-night chemist
Notausgang	emergency exit
Notfallstation	Accident and emergency unit
Notruf	emergency phone call
Notrufsäule	emergency telephone
Polizei	police

EMERGENCY TELEPHONE

	Austria	Germany	Switzerland
Ambulance	144	112	117
Fire	122	112	118
Police	133	110	117

CLOTHING SIZES

Waist/Chest measurements

Inches	28	30	32	34	36	38	40	42	44	46
cms	71	76	80	87	91	97	102	107	112	117

Women

Dresses

European	36	38	40	42	44	46
British	10	12	14	16	18	20
US	8	10	12	14	16	18

Shoes

European	36	37	38	39	40	41
British	4	4½	5	5½	6	6½
US	6	6½	7	7½	8	8½

Men

Jackets/Coats

European	46	48	50	52	54	56
British/US	36	38	40	42	44	46

Shirts

European	36	37	38	39	41	42	43
British/US	14	14½	15	15½	16	16½	17

Shoes

European	38	39	41	42	43	44	45
British	5	6	7	8	8½ /9	9½ /10	11
US	6½	7	8	8½	9	9½	10

NUMBERS

0	null	*nul*		11	elf	*elf*
1	eins	*I-ns*		12	zwölf	*tsvurlf*
2	zwei	*tsvy*		13	dreizehn	*drytsain*
	zwo	*tsvoh (on the phone)*		14	vierzehn	*feertsain*
3	drei	*dry*		15	fünfzehn	*fewnftsain*
4	vier	*feer*		16	sechzehn	*zekhtsain*
5	fünf	*fewnf*		17	siebzehn	*zeeptsain*
6	sechs	*zekhs*		18	achtzehn	*akhtsain*
7	sieben	*zeeben*		19	neunzehn	*noyntsain*
8	acht	*akht*		20	zwanzig	*tsvantsig*
9	neun	*noyn*		21	einundzwanzig	*I-n-*
10	zehn	*tsain*				*oont-tsvantsig*

i.e 'one-and-twenty'. All 'tens and units' numbers work like this.

30	dreißig	*drysig*
40	vierzig	*feertsig*
50	fünfzig	*fewnftsig*
60	sechzig	*zekhzig*
70	siebzig	*zeeptsig*
80	achtzig	*akhtsig*
90	neunzig	*noyntsig*
100	hundert	*hoondert*
101	hunderteins	*hoondert-yns*
200	zweihundert	*tsvy-hoondert*
1000	(ein)tausend	*(I-n) towzent*
1100	tausendeinhundert	*towzent-I-yn-hoondert*
2000	zweitausend	*tsvy-towzent*
1000000	eine Million	*I-ner miliohn*

1st	erste *airster*	once	einmal *I-nmaal*
2nd	zweite *tsvyter*	twice	zweimal *tsvymaal*
3rd	dritte *dritter*	10th	zehnte *tsainter*
4th	vierte *feerter*	20th	zwanzigste *tsvantsigster*

MONTHS

January	Januar *yanooaar*	July	Juli *yooli*
February	Februar *febrooaar*	August	August *owgoost*
March	März *mairts*	September	September *zeptember*
April	April *apreel*	October	Oktober *oktohber*
May	Mai *my*	November	November *nohvember*
June	Juni *yooni*	December	Dezember *daitsember*

DAYS

Sunday	Sonntag *zontaag*	Thursday	Donnerstag *donnerztaag*
Monday	Montag *mohntaag*	Friday	Freitag *frytaag*
Tuesday	Dienstag *deenstaag*	Saturday	Samstag *zamstaag* Sonnabend
Wednesday	Mittwoch *mitvokh*		(N. Germany) *zonaabent*

DATES

in (the) summer	im Sommer *im zommer*
What's the date today?	Der Wievielte ist heute? *dair veefeelter ist hoyter?*
It's the 3rd August	Es ist der dritte August *es ist dair dritter owgoost*
(at the) beginning/end of June	Anfang/Ende Juni *anfang/ender yooni*
(in the) middle of May	Mitte Mai *mitter my*
by/until July	bis Juli *bis yooli*
in October	im Oktober *im oktohber*
since August	seit August *zyt owgoost*
last/next month	letzten/nächsten Monat *letsten/nekhsten mohnaat*
on Tuesday	am Dienstag *am deenstaag*
last/next Friday	letzten/nächsten Freitag *letsten/nekhsten frytaag*
on Thursdays	Donnerstags *donnerztagz*
on 19th July	am neunzehnten Juli *am noyntsainten yooli*
today/tomorrow/yesterday	heute/morgen/gestern *hoyter/morgen/gestern*
two days ago	vor zwei Tagen *for tsvy taagen*

in four days' time	in vier Tagen
	in feer t<u>aa</u>gen
at the weekend	am Wochenende
	am v<u>o</u>khenender

TIME

What time is it?	Wie viel Uhr ist es?
	vee feel oor ist es?
It's…	Es ist…
	es ist…
…1.00	…ein Uhr
	I-n oor
…1.05	…fünf nach eins
	fewnf nakh I-ns
…1.15	…viertel nach eins
	f<u>ee</u>rtel nakh I-ns
…1.20	…zwanzig nach eins
	tsv<u>a</u>ntsig nakh eins
…1.30	…halb zwei
	halp tsvy
…1.50	….zehn vor zwei
	tsain for tsvy
…12.00 midday	…zwölf Uhr Mittag
midnight	Mitternacht
	tsv<u>ur</u>lf oor mittaag
	mitternakht
in the morning/afternoon/	morgens/nachmittags
evening	abends
	m<u>o</u>rgerns/n<u>a</u>kmitaagz/
	<u>aa</u>bents

In German 'half past' is 'half to' the next hour.

PUBLIC HOLIDAYS

• National holidays are shown: there are local variations.

	Austria = A	Germany = G	Switzerland = S
1 Jan	New Year's Day *Neujahr*	A	G	S
6 Jan	Epiphany *Dreikönigstag*	A		
1 May	Labour Day *Tag der Arbeit*	A	G	
17 June	German Unity Day *Tag der Deutschen Einheit*		G	
1 Aug	National Day *Nationalfeiertag*			S
15 Aug	Assumption *Mariä Himmelfahrt*	A		
26 Oct	National Day *Nationalfeiertag*	A		
1 Nov	All Saints' Day *Allerheiligen*	A		
8 Dec	Immaculate Conception *Mariä Empfängnis*	A		
25/6 Dec	Christmas *Weihnachten*	A	G	S

DICTIONARY

Numbers, days, seasons are given on pages 156–157.

Food starts on page 88.

Where appropriate, feminine versions of nouns are given in brackets, e.g. student: (die) Student(in) = der Student (m)/die Studentin (f).

The polite versions are indicated by (P) and the familiar by (F).

A

a ein/eine

about (number) ungefähr

    (time) gegen

above über

to accept nehmen

accident der Unfall

accommodation die Unterkunft

account das Konto

it aches es tut weh

across über

AIDS AIDS

adaptor der Adapter

address die Adresse

admission der Eintritt

adult der/die Erwachsene

after nach

afternoon der Nachmittag

again nochmal

against gegen

...ago vor...

air conditioning die Klimaanlage

airline die Fluglinie

by airmail per Luftpost

airport der Flughafen

alarm clock der Wecker

all (of them) alle

allergic to allergisch gegen

alone allein

already schon

also auch

always immer

am: I am ich bin

ambulance der Krankenwagen

America Amerika

American (adj.) amerikanisch

and und

animal das Tier

ankle der Knöchel

another (different) ein anderer

another (more) noch ein

to answer antworten

antibiotic das Antibiotikum

antiseptic cream die Wundsalbe

any (pl) einige

any more noch mehr

any others andere

apartment die Wohnung

appointment die Termin, die
                Verabredung

are: we/they are wir/sie sind
you are Sie sind (P), du bist (F)
arm der Arm
arrival die Ankunft
to arrive ankommen
art die Kunst
art gallery die Kunstgalerie
as soon as possible so bald wie
    möglich
ashtray der Aschenbecher
to ask fragen
  to ask for bitten um
aspirin das Aspirin
asthma das Asthma
at (place) an
    (time) um
    (someone's) bei
aunt die Tante
Australia Australien
Austria Österreich
automatic automatisch

B

baby das Baby
baby food die Babynahrung
back (body) der Rücken
    (direction) zurück
    at the back hinten
bad schlecht
bag die Tasche
baker's die Bäckerei
balcony der Balkon
ball der Ball
bandage der Verband

bank die Bank
bank note der (Geld)/Schein
bar (drink) die Bar
bath das Bad
  to have a bath ein Bad
    nehmen
bathroom das Badezimmer
battery die Batterie
beach der Strand
beard der Bart
beautiful schön
bed das Bett
bed linen die Bettwäsche
beer das Bier
before vor
to begin beginnen
beginner der Anfänger
behind hinter
Belgium Belgien
below unter
belt der Gürtel
best beste
better besser
between zwischen
bicycle das Fahrrad
big groß
bill die Rechnung
birthday der Geburtstag
bite (insect) der Stich/der Biss
bitter bitter
black schwarz
blanket die Decke
to bleed bluten

blister   die Blase

blood   das Blut

blood pressure   der Blutdruck

blouse   die Bluse

blue   blau

boat   das Schiff, das Boot

body   der Körper

to boil   kochen

bone   der Knochen

bonnet (car)   die Motorhaube

book   das Buch

to book   reservieren

booking office   der Reservierungsschalter

boot (car)   der Kofferraum
(shoe)   der Stiefel

born: I was b. in…   ich bin in … geboren

border   die Grenze

boring   langweilig

to borrow   leihen

both   beide

bottle   die Flasche

bottle-opener   der Flaschenöffner

bottom (body)   der Hintern

bowl   die Schüssel

box   die Schachtel

box office   die Kasse

boy   der Junge

boyfriend   der Freund

bra   der Büstenhalter/BH

bracelet   das Armband

to brake   bremsen

brakes   die Bremse

brandy   der Weinbrand

bread   das Brot

to break   brechen

breakdown   die Panne

breakdown truck   der Abschleppwagen

breakfast   das Frühstück

breast   die Brust

to breathe   atmen

bridge   die Brücke

to bring   bringen

British (adj)   britisch

broken (bone)   gebrochen
(machine)   kaputt

brother   der Bruder

brown   braun

bruise   die Quetschung

building   das Gebäude

burn (injury)   die Brandwunde

to burn   brennen

bus   der Bus

bus station   der Busbahnhof

business   das Geschäft
on…   geschäftlich

busy (café)   voll
(lots to do)   beschäftigt

but   aber

butane gas   das Butangas

butcher's   die Fleischerei/ Metzgerei

butter   die Butter

button   der Knopf
to buy   kaufen
by (author, maker)   von
   (time)   bis
   (next to)   neben

C

cable car   die Drahtseilbahn
café   das Café
cake   der Kuchen
calculator   der Rechner
call (summon)   rufen
   (phone)   anrufen
   (what's this called?)   Wie
                     heißt das?
calm   ruhig
camera   der Fotoapparat
to camp   zelten
campsite   der Campingplatz
can (able to)   können
   (of food)   die Dose
canal   der Kanal
Canada   Kanada
to cancel   annullieren
candle   der Kerze
canoe   das Kanu
car   das Auto/der Wagen
car park   der Parkplatz
caravan   der Wohnwagen
carriage (rail)   der Wagen
cash   das Bargeld
cash desk   die Kasse
cash dispenser   der Geld-
                   automat

to cash   einlösen
castle   das Schloss, die Burg
cathedral   der Dom, die
                   Kathedrale
CD player   der CD-Spieler
cellar   der Keller
centre   die Mitte
chain   die Kette
chair   der Stuhl
Channel Tunnel   der Kanaltunnel
change (money)   das Kleingeld
to change
   (alter)   ändern
   (money)   wechseln
   (trains)   umsteigen
charge   die Gebühr/der Tarif
cheap   billig
to check   kontrollieren
   to check in   einchecken
   to check out   abreisen
checkout (shop)   die Kasse
checkup (medical)
                   die Untersuchung
cheers!   Prost!
cheese   der Käse
chemist   die Apotheke/ Drogerie
cheque   der Scheck
cheque book   das Scheckbuch
cheque card   die Scheckkarte
chest   die Brust
child   das Kind
chips   die Pommes frites
chocolate   die Schokolade

to choose wählen
Christian name der Vorname
church die Kirche
cider der Apfelwein
cigar die Zigarre
cigarette die Zigarette
cigarette lighter das Feuerzeug
cinema das Kino
circle (theatre) der Rang
city die Stadt
class die Klasse
clean sauber
to clean reinigen
clear klar
cling film die Lebensmittelfolie
cloakroom die Garderobe
clock die Uhr
to close schließen
closed geschlossen
cloth der Stoff
clothes die Kleider
cloud die Wolke
clutch (car) die Kupplung
coach der Bus
coat der Mantel
coathanger der Kleiderbügel
coffee der Kaffee
coin die Münze
cold (illness) die Erkältung
       (adj) kalt
colour die Farbe
comb der Kamm
to come kommen

comfortable bequem
Compact Disc die CD
compartment das Abteil
complicated kompliziert
concert das Konzert
concert hall die Konzerthalle
conditioner die Haarspülung
condom das Kondom
conference die Konferenz
conference centre
          die Kongresshalle
to confirm bestätigen
congratulations! herzlichen
          Glückwunsch!
connection (transport)
          der Anschluss
constipation die Verstopfung
contact lens die Kontaktlinse
to contain enthalten
contraceptive
          das Verhütungsmittel
contract der Vertrag
to cook kuchen
corkscrew der Korkenzieher
to cost kosten
cot das Kinderbett
cotton die Baumwolle
cotton wool die Watte
cough der Husten
country das Land
cousin der (die) Cousin(e)
cramp der Krampf
cream (milk) die Sahne

credit card die Kreditkarte
crisps die Chips
to cross überqueren
cross-country skiing
        der Langlauf
crossroads die Kreuzung
crowded voll, überfüllt
cup die Tasse
cupboard der Schrank
currency die Währung
current (electric, water)
        der Strom
curtain der Vorhang
customs die Zollabfertigung
to cut schneiden
cut (wound) die Schnittwunde
cycling das Radfahren

D

damp feucht
to dance tanzen
dangerous gefährlich
dark dunkel
daughter die Tochter
day der Tag
dead tot
deaf taub
deckchair der Liegestuhl
deep tief
delay die Verspätung
to deliver liefern
Denmark Dänemark
dentist der Zahnarzt
denture die Zahnprothese

deodorant das Deodorant
department die Abteilung
department store das Kaufhaus
departure die Abfahrt,
        der Abflug
to leave a deposit
        eine Sicherheit hinterlegen
dessert der Nachtisch
detour (road) die Umleitung
to develop entwickeln
diabetic der (die) Diabetiker(in)
dialling code die Vorwahl
diamond der Diamant
diarrhoea der Durchfall
dictionary das Wörterbuch
diesel das Diesel
different (other) andere
        (various) verschiedene
difficult schwierig
dining car die Speisewagen
dining room (hotel)
        der Speisesaal
dinner (evening meal)
        das Abendessen
direct direkt
to direct (to) den Weg zeigen
direction die Richtung
dirty schmutzig
disabled person
        der/die Behinderte
to dislocate verrenken
dissatisfied unzufrieden
divorced geschieden
to do machen

doctor der Arzt
door die Tür
dormitory der Schlafraum
double room das Doppelzimmer
down hinunter
downhill skiing der Abfahrtslauf
downstairs unten
dress das Kleid
drink das Getränk
to drink trinken
drinking water das Trinkwasser
to drip (tap) tropfen
to drive fahren
driver der Fahrer
driving licence der Führerschein
drunk betrunken
dry trocken
dry cleaners
      die chemische Reinigung
duty-free zollfrei
duvet die Steppdecke

E

each jeder/jede/jedes
ear das Ohr
early früh
east der Osten/(adj) östlich
easy leicht
to eat essen
either of them es ist egal
either ... or ...
      entweder ... oder ...
electric(al) elektrisch
electricity der Stromanschluss

e-mail (address)
   der E-Mail (die E-Mail Adresse)
embarrassing peinlich
emergency der Notfall
empty leer
end das Ende
to end enden
engaged (couple) verlobt
      (in use) besetzt
engine (car) der Motor
England England
enlargement die Vergrößerung
English (adj) englisch
   I'm English ich bin Engländer
enough genug
entertainment die Unterhaltung
entrance der Eingang
entrance fee der Eintritt
envelope der Umschlag
equipment die Ausrüstung
escalator die Rolltreppe
especially besonders
Europe Europa
EU die Europäische Union
evening der Abend
evening meal das Abendessen
every/everyone jeder
everything alles
everywhere überall
exact(ly) genau
for example zum Beispiel
except (for) außer
to exchange (goods)
      umtauschen

exchange rate der Wechselkurs
excursion der Ausflug
exhaust pipe der Auspuff
exhibition die Ausstellung
exit (building) der Ausgang
   (motorway) die Ausfahrt
to expect erwarten
expensive teuer
to explain erklären
extra zusätzlich
eye das Auge

F

face das Gesicht
factory die Fabrik
faint (feeling) schwach
fair (funfair) der Jahrmarkt
to fall fallen
family die Familie
famous berühmt
fan belt der Keilriemen
far weit
fare der Fahrpreis
farm der Bauernhof
fashionable modisch
fast schnell
fat (on food) das Fett
  fat dick
father der Vater
favourite Lieblings-
fax das Fax
  fax machine das Faxgerät
  to fax
    faxen/ ein Telefax schicken

I feel... ich fühle mich...
ferry die Fähre
to fetch holen
fever das Fieber
a few ein paar
fiancé(e) der (die) Verlobte
field das Feld
to fill füllen
  to fill in (form) ausfüllen
filling (tooth) die Plombe
film der Film
to find finden
fine (money) die Geldstrafe
  (OK) gut/OK
finger der Finger
fire das Feuer, der Brand
fire brigade die Feuerwehr
firm (company) die Firma
first erster
first-aid kit der Verbandkasten
first name der Vorname
fish der Fisch
fishing das Angeln
fishing permit der Angelschein
fishing tackle das Angelzeug
to fit passen
fizzy mit Kohlensäure
flash (photo) der Blitz
flat (battery) leer
  (apartment) die Wohnung
  (shape) flach
flight der Flug
flight number die Flugnummer

floor (storey) der Stock

florist das Blumengeschäft

flour das Mehl

flower die Blume

flu die Grippe

fly (insect) die Fliege

to fly fliegen

fog der Nebel

food das Essen

food poisoning
die Lebensmittelvergiftung

foot der Fuß

on foot zu Fuß

football der Fußball

footpath der Fußweg

for für

(+ past time) seit

(+ future time) für

foreigner
der (die) Ausländer(in)

forest der Wald

to forget vergessen

fork die Gabel

form das Formular

fortnight zwei Wochen

fountain der Brunnen

fracture der Bruch

France Frankreich

free kostenlos

freezer der Gefrierschrank

to freeze frieren

French (adj) französisch

fresh frisch

friend der (die) Freund(in)

friendly freundlich

from von, aus

in front of vor

fruit das Obst

fruit juice der Fruchtsaft

to fry braten

full voll

I'm full Ich bin satt

full board die Vollpension

full up (hotel) belegt

funny komisch

furniture die Möbel

fuse die Sicherung

G

game das Spiel

garage (repairs) die Werkstatt

garden der Garten

gas das Gas

gate das Tor

gay (homosexual) schwul

gear der Gang

gear box das Getriebe

genuine echt

German (adj) deutsch

(noun) der/die Deutsche

(lang) Deutsch

Germany Deutschland

to get (become) werden

(fetch) holen

(obtain) bekommen

(train) nehmen

to get on (bus) einsteigen

to get off (bus) aussteigen
to get to kommen nach/zu
to get to know kennen lernen
to get up aufstehen
girl das Mädchen
girlfriend die Freundin
to give geben
glass das Glas
glasses die Brille
gloves die Handschuhe
glue der Klebstoff
to go gehen, fahren
to go out ausgehen
gold das Gold
golf das Golf
golf course der Golfplatz
good gut
good-bye (in person)
Auf Wiedersehen
(phone)
Auf Wiederhören
grass das Gras
greasy fettig
Great Britain Großbritannien
green grün
greengrocer's
die Gemüsehandlung
grey grau
grocer's
das Lebensmittelgeschäft
ground floor das Erdgeschoss
group die Gruppe
guarantee die Garantie

guide der Führer/die Führerin
guide book der Reiseführer
guitar die Gitarre
gum (teeth) das Zahnfleisch

H

hair die Haare
hairbrush die Haarbürste
hairdresser's der Friseur
hairdryer der Föhn
half die Hälfte, halb
half board die Halbpension
half price zum halben Preis
hand die Hand
hand luggage das Handgepäck
handbag die Handtasche
handkerchief das Taschentuch
happy glücklich
harbour der Hafen
hard (surface) hart
hat der Hut
to have haben
hay fever der Heuschnupfen
he er
head der Kopf
headache Kopfschmerzen
headlights die Scheinwerfer
healthy gesund
to hear hören
heart das Herz
heart attack der Herzinfarkt
heating die Heizung
heavy schwer

heel (shoe) der Absatz

hello! hallo! Guten Tag

to help helfen

help! Hilfe!

her sie/ihr

here hier

high hoch

hill der Berg, der Hügel

to hire mieten

his/him sein/ihn/ihm

history die Geschichte

to hitchhike trampen

HIV positive HIV-positiv

to hold halten

hole das Loch

holidays der Urlaub

(public) der Feiertag

at home zu Hause

(back) home (travel) nach Hause

home address der Wohnort

honest ehrlich

horn (car) die Hupe

horrible schrecklich

horse das Pferd

horse-riding das Pferdereiten

hospital das Krankenhaus

hot heiß

hotel das Hotel

hour die Stunde

how? wie?

how about...?

wie wäre es mit... ?

how far? wie weit?

how many? wie viele?

how much? wie viel?

hunger der Hunger

I'm hungry ich habe Hunger

hurry up! beeilen Sie sich!

it hurts es tut weh

husband der Mann

I

I ich

ice das Eis

ice-cream das Eis

ice-rink das Eisstadion

ice-skating das Eislaufen

ill krank

immediate(ly) sofort

important wichtig

impossible unmöglich

in in

including inbegriffen

indicator (car) der Blinker

indigestion

die Magenverstimmung

infection die Infektion

information die Auskunft

information office

das Informationsbüro

injection die Spritze

injured verletzt

injury die Verletzung

insect repellant

der Insektenschutz

inside drinnen

instead (of that) statt(dessen)

insurance die Versicherung
interesting interessant
international international
internet das Internet
interpreter der (die) Dolmetscher(in)
to introduce vorstellen
invitation die Einladung
to invite einladen
Ireland Irland
to iron bügeln
is: he/she/it is er/sie/es ist
island die Insel
it es
Italian (adj) italienisch
Italy Italien

J

jacket die Jacke
jam die Marmelade
to jam (get stuck) klemmen
jar das Glas
jersey der Pullover
jeweller's der Juwelier
jewellery der Schmuck
job die Arbeit
to go jogging joggen gehen
joke der Witz
journey die Reise
juice der Saft
just (only) nur

K

to keep behalten

key der Schlüssel
kind nett, freundlich
kitchen die Küche
knee das Knie
knife das Messer
to knock klopfen
to know (about) wissen
(person, place) kennen
I (don't) know Ich weiß (nicht)

L

label das Etikett
lady die Dame/die Frau
lake der See
land das Land
to land landen
landscape die Landschaft
language die Sprache
large groß
last letzte
to last dauern
at last! endlich
late spät
to laugh lachen
launderette der Waschsalon
laxative das Abführmittel
lead-free bleifrei
to learn lernen
at least mindestens
leather das Leder
to leave (something) lassen
(depart) abfahren
to leave luggage das Gepäck einstellen

left linke
  to the left links
leg das Bein
lemonade die Limonade
length die Länge
less weniger
letter der Brief
library die Bibliothek
licence die Erlaubnis
  (driving) der Führerschein
to lie down sich hinlegen
life belt der Rettungsring
lift der Fahrstuhl/Aufzug
light (colour) hell
  (not heavy) leicht
  (lamp) die Lampe
light bulb die Birne
like (similar) ähnlich
  I like... ...gefällt mir
    ich mag...
  it's like... es ist wie...
like this so
line die Linie
lip die Lippe
lipsalve die Lippensalbe
lipstick der Lippenstift
to listen hören
litre der/das Liter
litter der Abfall
little klein
(a) little ein wenig
to live wohnen
loaf (of bread) das Brot

local aus der Gegend
long lang
to look sehen
  to look for suchen
  to have a look (in shop)
    sich umsehen
loose (clothes) weit
  (screw) locker
to lose verlieren
to get lost sich verirren
lost property office
    das Fundbüro
a lot (of) viel/viele
loud laut
lounge (hotel) die Lounge
  (house) das Wohnzimmer
to love lieben
lovely schön
low niedrig
luck: good luck! viel Glück!
luggage das Gepäck
luggage trolley der Kofferkuli
lunch das Mittagessen

M

machine die Maschine
made of aus
magazine die Zeitschrift
mail die Post
main Haupt-
to make machen
man der Mann
manager der Manager
many viele

map (of country) die Karte
   (of town) der Stadtplan
market der Markt
married verheiratet
mass (church) die Messe
match (game) der Wettkampf
   (lighter) das Streichholz
matter: it doesn't matter
              es macht nichts
mattress die Matratze
material der Stoff
may I? kann ich?
meal das Essen
mean: what does ... mean?
            Was bedeutet ...?
to measure Maß nehmen
meat das Fleisch
mechanic der Mechaniker
medical ärztlich
medical certificate
        der Krankenschein
medical insurance
        die Krankenkasse
medicine das Medikament
medium-sized mittelgroß
to meet treffen
member das Mitglied
to mend flicken, reparieren
menu die Speisekarte
message die Nachricht
middle die Mitte
migraine die Migräne
milk die Milch
mine: it's mine es gehört mir

mineral water
        das Mineralwasser
minute die Minute
mirror der Spiegel
to miss (train) verpassen
mistake der Fehler
mixed gemischt
mobile phone das Handy
modern modern
moment der Augenblick
money das Geld
month der Monat
monument das Denkmal
more mehr
morning der Morgen
most(ly) meist(ens)
mother die Mutter
motor boat das Motorboot
motorbike das Motorrad
motorway die Autobahn
mountain der Berg
mountaineering das Bergsteigen
moustache der Schnurrbart
mouth der Mund
to move bewegen
Mr Herr
Mrs/Ms Frau
much viel
muscle der Muskel
museum das Museum
music die Musik
must: I must ich muss
my mein

N

nail der Nagel
nail clippers die Nagelzange
nail polish der Nagellack
name der Name
napkin die Serviette
nappy die Windel
narrow eng
nationality die Nationalität
near nah
  near here hier in der Nähe
nearest nächste
neck der Hals
to need brauchen
there's no need
        das ist nicht nötig
needle die Nadel
neither of them
        keiner von beiden
neither … nor … weder… noch …
Netherlands die Niederlande
never nie
new neu
news die Nachrichten
newsagent's der Zeitungsladen
newspaper die Zeitung
New Zealand Neuseeland
next nächste
  next time nächstes Mal
  next to neben
nice (thing) nett/schön
  (person) sympathisch
night die Nacht

night club das Nachtlokal
no nein
I've no idea
        Ich habe keine Ahnung
noisy laut
non-alcoholic alkoholfrei
none keine
non-smoker der Nichtraucher
normally normalerweise
north der Norden/(adj) nördlich
Norway Norwegen
nose die Nase
nosebleed das Nasenbluten
not nicht
not yet noch nicht
nothing nichts
now jetzt
number (of house, etc)
        die Nummer
  (quantity) der Zahl
number plate
        das Nummernschild
nurse die Krankenschwester
nut (fruit) die Nuss

O

occupied besetzt
of von
office das Büro
often oft
oil das Öl
ointment die Salbe
old alt
on an, auf

once einmal

one-way street
                die Einbahnstraße

one-way (ticket) einfach

only nur

open offen

to open öffnen

opening times (shops, museums)
                Öffnungszeiten

    (business) Geschäftszeiten

opera die Oper

opposite gegenüber

optician der Optiker

or oder

orchestra das Orchester

to order bestellen

other andere

our unser

out: he's out er ist nicht da

out of order außer Betrieb

outside draußen

over über

over there da drüben

to overtake überholen

P

to pack einpacken

packet die Schachtel

page die Seite

pain der Schmerz

painkiller das Schmerzmittel

paint die Farbe

to paint malen

painting das Bild

pair das Paar

pale blass

palace der Palast/das Schloss

paper das Papier

paperback das Taschenbuch

parcel das Paket

pardon? wie bitte?

parents die Eltern

park der Park

to park parken

parking disc die Parkscheibe

parking meter die Parkuhr

party die Party

pass der Pass

passenger
        der Fahrgast/der Passagier

passport der Pass

pastry das Gebäck

patient der (die) Patient(in)

to pay (be)zahlen

pedestrian der Fußgänger

pen (ball-point) der Kuli

    (fountain) der Füller

pencil der Bleistift

penfriend
            der (die) Brieffreund(in)

penicillin das Penizillin

pensioner der (die) Rentner(in)

people die Leute

per pro

performance die Aufführung

perfume das Parfüm

period pains
            Menstruationsschmerzen

permit die Genehmigung

perhaps vielleicht

personal persönlich

petrol das Benzin

petrol station die Tankstelle

phone das Telefon

to phone anrufen

phone box die Telefonzelle

phonecard die Telefonkarte

phone number die Telefonnummer

photo das Foto

photocopy die Fotokopie

to photograph fotografieren

phrasebook der Sprachführer

to pick someone up abholen

pickpocket der Taschendieb

picnic das Picknick

picture das Bild

piece das Stück

pill die Pille, die Tablette

pink rosa

pipe die Pfeife

place der Ort

place of birth der Geburtsort

places of interest die Sehenswürdigkeiten

plan der Plan

to plan planen

plane das Flugzeug

plaster (sticking) das Pflaster

plastic das Plastik

plastic bag die Plastiktüte

plate der Teller

platform (station) der Bahnsteig/das Gleis

play (theatre) das Stück

to play spielen

please bitte

plug (electric) der Stecker

(sink) der Stöpsel

pocket die Tasche

to point zeigen

poison das Gift

poisoning die Vergiftung

police die Polizei

police station das Polizeirevier

police (wo)man der (die) Polizist(in)

port der Hafen

portable tragbar

porter der Gepäckträger

portion die Portion

possible/possibly möglich

possibly vielleicht

post die Post

to post aufgeben

post office die Post

postbox der Briefkasten

postcard die Postkarte, die Ansichtskarte

poster das Poster

pound (money/weight) das Pfund

powder der Puder

to prefer/I prefer Ich mag lieber

pregnant schwanger
prescription das Rezept
present das Geschenk
pretty hübsch
price der Preis
private privat
probably wahrscheinlich
problem das Problem
processing (film) die Entwicklung
profession der Beruf
programme das Programm
pub das Lokal/die Wirtschaft
public öffentlich
to pull ziehen
pullover der Pullover
puncture das Loch
punctual pünktlich
purse das Portemonnaie
to push (button) drücken
(car) schieben
pushchair der Kinderwagen
to put stellen, legen
pyjamas der Schlafanzug

Q

quality die Qualität
question die Frage
to queue Schlange stehen
quick(ly) schnell
quiet ruhig
quite (fairly) ziemlich
(completely) ganz

R

radiator (car) der Kühler
(room) der Heizkörper
radio das Radio
by rail mit der Bahn
to rain regnen
raincoat der Regenmantel
rash (medical) der Ausschlag
to read lesen
ready fertig
real echt
rear hinten/Hinter-
receipt die Quittung
receive bekommen
receptionist der Empfangschef
to recommend empfehlen
red rot
refill (pen) die Ersatzmine
refreshments die Erfrischungen
to give a refund das Geld zurückgeben
region die Gegend
registration form das Anmeldeformular
relative der/die Verwandte
relax sich entspannen
religion die Religion
to rent mieten
repair die Reparatur
to repair reparieren
to repeat wiederholen
to reserve reservieren

restaurant
das Restaurant/die Gaststätte
return ticket hin und zurück
to return (give) zurückgeben
(travel) zurückfahren
reverse charge call
das R-Gespräch
to the right rechts
right (correct) richtig
ring der Ring
to ring (doorbell) klingeln
(phone someone) anrufen
ripe reif
river der Fluss
road die Straße
road sign das Verkehrsschild
romantic romantisch
room das Zimmer
(space) der Platz
room service der Zimmerservice
rope das Seil
round rund
route die Strecke
rowing boat das Ruderboot
rubber (material) der Gummi
rubbish der Abfall, der Müll
rucksack der Rucksack
ruins die Ruinen
ruler (measure) das Lineal
to run laufen

S
sad traurig
safe ungefährlich
(strongbox) der Safe
safety pin die Sicherheitsnadel
to sail segeln
sale der Schlussverkauf
for sale zu verkaufen
same: the same das Gleiche
same again, please
noch einmal das Gleiche, bitte
saucepan der Kochtopf
sausage die Wurst
to say sagen
What did you say? Wie, bitte?
How do you say ...?
Wie sagt man ...?
scarf der Schal
school die Schule
science die Naturwissenschaften
scissors die Schere
Scotland Schottland
screwdriver der Schraubenzieher
sea die See
seat der Platz
seat belt der Sicherheitsgurt
second (time) die Sekunde
second-hand
gebraucht, antiquarisch
to see sehen
to sell verkaufen
sellotape der Tesafilm
to send schicken

separate(ly) getrennt
service (church)
   der Gottesdienst
   (restaurant)
   die Bedienung
services (motorway)
   die Raststätte
to sew nähen
shampoo das Shampoo
sharp scharf
to shave sich rasieren
shaver der Rasierapparat
shaving cream die Rasiercreme
she sie
ship das Schiff
shirt das Hemd
shoe der Schuh
   shoelace der Schnürsenkel
   shoe polish die Schuhcreme
   shoe repairer's
      der Schuh-Reparaturdienst
shop das Geschäft, der Laden
to go shopping einkaufen gehen
shop window das Schaufenster
shopping centre
      das Einkaufszentrum
short kurz
shorts die Shorts
shoulder die Schulter
to show zeigen
shower (bath) die Dusche
   (rain) der Schauer
shower gel das Duschgel
shut geschlossen

to shut schließen
shutter (window)
   der Fensterladen
sick (ill) krank
   sickness (illness) die Krankheit
   sick: I feel sick mir ist übel
   I've been sick
      ich habe mich übergeben
side die Seite
sightseeing die Besichtigung
sights die Sehenswürdigkeiten
sign das Schild
to sign unterschreiben
signature die Unterschrift
silk die Seide
silver das Silber
simple einfach
since seit
to sing singen
single (ticket) einfach
   (unmarried) ledig
single room das Einzelzimmer
sister die Schwester
size (clothes) die Größe
   (shoes) die Nummer
skates Schlittschuhe
to skate Eis laufen
skating rink die Eisbahn
skis Skier
to ski Ski laufen
ski binding die Skibindung
ski-boot der Skistiefel
ski-lift der Skilift

skin die Haut
skirt der Rock
sky der Himmel
to sleep schlafen
sleeping bag der Schlafsack
sleeping car der Schlafwagen
slice die Scheibe
slippers Hausschuhe
slow(ly) langsam
small klein
to smoke rauchen
smoker der Raucher
snack der Imbiss
snow der Schnee
to snow schneien
soap die Seife
socks die Socken
socket (electric) die Steckdose
soft weich
soft drink
       ein alkoholfreies Getränk
sole (shoe) die Sohle
some (pl) einige
someone jemand
something (else) etwas (anderes)
sometimes manchmal
son der Sohn
song das Lied/der Song
soon bald
I'm sorry Entschuldigung
sour sauer
south der Süden/(adj) südlich
souvenir das Andenken

Spain Spanien
Spanish spanisch
spanner der Schraubenschlüssel
spare part das Ersatzteil
spare tyre der Ersatzreifen
spark plug die Zündkerze
to speak sprechen
special offer das Sonderangebot
speciality die Spezialität
spectator der Zuschauer
speed die Geschwindigkeit
to spell buchstabieren
to spend (money) ausgeben
      (time) verbringen
spoon der Löffel
sport der Sport
square (shape) viereckig
      (in town) der Platz
stadium das Stadion
stain der Fleck
stairs die Treppe
stalls (theatre) das Parkett
stamp (postage) die Briefmarke
to start beginnen
    (car) anspringen
station (rail) der Bahnhof
    (tube) die Station
to stay (on holiday) wohnen
    (remain) bleiben
to steal stehlen
steering wheel das Lenkrad
sting der Stich
stockings die Strümpfe

stolen gestohlen
stomach der Magen
stop (bus) die Haltestelle
stop! halt!
to stop (halt) halten
        (doing) aufhören
storm das Unwetter
straight direkt/gerade
straight on geradeaus
street die Straße
  street map der Stadtplan
string der Bindfaden
strong stark
student der (die) Student(in)
to study studieren
stupid dumm
sugar der Zucker
suit (clothes) der Anzug
suitcase der Koffer
sun die Sonne
to sunbathe in der Sonne liegen
sunburn der Sonnenbrand
sunglasses die Sonnenbrille
sunny: it's sunny es ist sonnig
sunshade der Sonnenschirm
sun-tan cream das Sonnenöl
supermarket der Supermarkt
supper (evening meal)
                das Abendessen
surcharge der Zuschlag
surname der Nachname
to swallow schlucken
Sweden Schweden

sweet (flavour) süß
sweets die Bonbons
to swim schwimmen
swimming pool
                das Schwimmbad
  (indoor) das Hallenbad
  (outdoor) das Freibad
swimming trunks die Badehose
swimsuit der Badeanzug
Swiss (adj) schweizerisch
switch der Schalter
Switzerland die Schweiz
swollen geschwollen
synagogue die Synagoge

T
table der Tisch
to take nehmen
  (time) dauern
take-away (food)
                zum Mitnehmen
take off der Abflug
to talk sprechen, reden
tall groß
tampon der Tampon
tap der Hahn
taxi das Taxi
taxi rank der Taxistand
tea der Tee
tea bag der Teebeutel
teaspoon der Teelöffel
technology die Technik
television der Fernseher
to tell sagen

temperature die Temperatur
  (fever) das Fieber
temporary provisorisch
tent das Zelt
tent peg der Hering
tent pole die Zeltstange
tennis das Tennis
tennis court der Tennisplatz
tennis racket der Tennisschläger
terminus die Endstation
terrible schrecklich
to text simsen/texten
than als
thank you danke
that (one) der/die/das
the der/die/das
theatre das Theater
their ihr
then dann
there dort
there is/there are es gibt
thermometer das Thermometer
these diese
they sie
thick dick
thief der Dieb
thin dünn
to think (opinion) meinen
  I think so Ich glaube schon
  I'll think about it
          Ich überlege es mir
I'm thirsty Ich habe Durst
this (one) dieser/diese/dieses

this is ... das ist ...
throat der Hals
  throat pastille
                  die Halspastille
through durch
thumb der Daumen
thunderstorm das Gewitter
ticket (bus) der Fahrschein
       (plane) die Flugkarte
       (rail) die Fahrkarte
       (entrance)
                  die (Eintritts) Karte
       (dry cleaner's) der Zettel
ticket office
                  der Fahrkartenschalter
tide (high) die Flut
     (low) die Ebbe
tie die Krawatte
tight eng
tights die Strumpfhose
till die Kasse
time (measure) die Zeit
     (occasion) das Mal
next time nächstes Mal
on time pünktlich
timetable der Fahrplan
tin (can) die Dose
tin opener der Dosenöffner
tired müde
tissues Papiertücher
to (town, country) nach
     (building, road) zu
tobacco der Tabak
tobacconist's der Tabakladen

today heute

toe die Zehe

together zusammen

toilet die Toilette

toilet paper das Toilettenpapier

toiletries die Toilettenartikel

toll die Gebühr, die Maut

tomorrow morgen

tomorrow morning morgen früh

tongue die Zunge

tonight heute Abend

too (much) zu
(also) auch

tooth der Zahn
toothache die Zahnschmerzen
toothbrush die Zahnbürste
toothpaste die Zahnpasta

torch die Taschenlampe

to touch berühren

tour
die Rundfahrt, der Rundgang

tourist der Tourist

tourist office das
Fremdenverkehrsbüro/
das Informationsbüro

to tow abschleppen

towards gegen

towel das Handtuch

tower der Turm

town die Stadt

town centre die Innenstadt

toy das Spielzeug

traffic (road) der Verkehr

traffic jam der Stau

traffic light die Ampel

trailer der Anhänger

train der Zug
by train mit der Bahn

transfer (bank) die Überweisung

to translate übersetzen

to travel reisen

travel agent das Reisebüro

travel sickness
die Reisekrankheit

traveller's cheque
der Reisescheck

tree der Baum

trip (excursion) der Ausflug

trousers die Hose

true wahr
that's true das stimmt

to try (attempt) versuchen
(sample) probieren

to try on anprobieren

tube die Tube

twice zweimal

twin beds zwei Einzelbetten

to type tippen

tyre der Reifen

U

umbrella der Regenschirm

uncle der Onkel

unconscious bewusstlos

under unter

underground die U-Bahn

underpants die Unterhose

to understand verstehen

underwear die Unterwäsche

United States die Vereinigten Staaten

university die Universität

until bis

unusual ungewöhnlich

up hinauf

upset stomach die Magenverstimmung

upstairs oben

urgent dringend

to use benutzen

useful nützlich

usual gewöhnlich

V

vacancy ein freies Zimmer
'no vacancies' 'belegt'

vacant frei

vacuum cleaner der Staubsauger

valley das Tal

VAT MwSt (Mehrwertsteuer)

vegetables das Gemüse

vegetarian vegetarisch

very sehr

video cassette die Videocassette

video recorder der Videorecorder

view die Aussicht

village das Dorf

vineyard der Weinberg

visit der Besuch

to visit besuchen

visitor der/die Besucher/in

W

to wait warten

waiter der Kellner/Herr Ober!

waiting room der Wartesaal

waitress die Kellnerin/Bedienung!

Wales Wales

to go for a walk einen Spaziergang machen

to walk zu Fuß gehen

walking (hiking) das Wandern

wallet die Brieftasche

to want wollen

to wash sich waschen

wash basin das Waschbecken

washing powder das Waschpulver

washing-up liquid das Spülmittel

wasp die Wespe

watch (clock) die Armbanduhr

to watch sehen

water das Wasser

waterfall der Wasserfall

waterproof wasserdicht

waterskiing das Wasserskilaufen

we wir

to wear tragen

weather das Wetter

weather forecast der Wetterbericht

website die Webseite

week die Woche
weekend das Wochenende
well (feeling) gut
   (healthy) wohl
   (water) der Brunnen
west der Westen/(adj) westlich
wet nass
what? was?
wheel das Rad
wheelchair der Rollstuhl
when? wann?
where? wo?
which?
      welcher/welche/welches?
white weiß
who? wer?
whole ganz
why? warum?
wide breit
wife die Frau
wind der Wind
window das Fenster
windscreen
      die Windschutzscheibe
windscreen wiper
      der Scheibenwischer
windsurfing das Windsurfen
wine der Wein
with mit
without ohne
woman die Dame/die Frau
wonderful wunderbar

wood (forest) der Wald
   (material) das Holz
wool die Wolle
word das Wort
to work (job) arbeiten
   (function) funktionieren
worse schlechter
to wrap einpacken
wrist das Handgelenk
to write schreiben
writing paper das Schreibpapier
wrong falsch

Y
year das Jahr
yellow gelb
yes ja
yesterday gestern
yet: not yet noch nicht
you du (F)/Sie (P)
young jung
your dein (F)/Ihr (P)
youth hostel die Jugendherberge

Z
zip der Reißverschluss
zoo der Zoo